Lose Weight With Apple Vinegar

Get the ideal body the easy way: Using powers of apple vinegar to lose weight with the successful four-week diet program.

This book is intended as an education devise to keep you informed of the latest medical knowledge. It is not intended to serve as a substitute for changing the treatment advice of your doctor. You should never make a medical change without first consulting with your doctor.

Contents

Preface

Good Food and its Consequences

During the last several decades, life has improved for people in industrial nations: They have plenty to eat. First the war generation wanted to fill their bellies after years of hunger, then international restaurants became fashionable. Eating out became a status symbol. Feasting became the motto of the last decades.

Slowly the people became saturated - and fatter: Obesity and being overweight became dominating topics. Soon dozens and dozens of diets, weight loss programs and slimness guides hit the bookshelves. Each diet promised fast weight loss - but in the long run, none of the diets kept their promises.

Apple Vinegar Offers You New Chances

Many people try desperately to recover those pretty and slim bodies from their teens. They fight fiercely to lose pounds, lead a secret war against the scale, and still do not succeed - for they choose the wrong way. Apple vinegar, on the other hand, makes losing weight easy, very effective, and works in a natural way.

Apple vinegar becomes an ally of your body, and balances the organism. Apple vinegar activates all natural mechanisms that can dislodge the fat and decrease it. Its fat-fighting effect has made apple vinegar a proven medicine for a long time.

Apple vinegar is an old and proven medicine. Its fat- fighting effect makes it extremely suitable for weight loss programs.

Desire for Healthy Food

You will find numerous suggestions for recipes with apple vinegar in this book. Because a healthy diet does not demand sacrificing or reducing your consumption of healthy food, it can also be enjoyable to your taste buds. Nonetheless, you should also choose your foods for their diet-physiological aspects. Therefore, an important chapter of this guide is called "Healthy Food with Apple Vinegar".

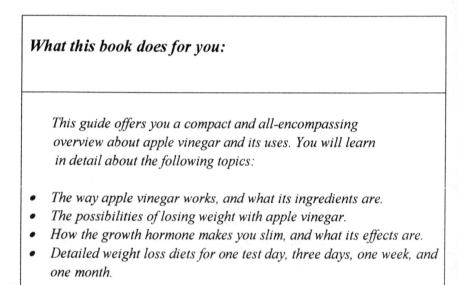

What this book does for you:

This guide offers you a compact and all-encompassing overview about apple vinegar and its uses. You will learn in detail about the following topics:

- *The way apple vinegar works, and what its ingredients are.*
- *The possibilities of losing weight with apple vinegar.*
- *How the growth hormone makes you slim, and what its effects are.*
- *Detailed weight loss diets for one test day, three days, one week, and one month.*

Many people consider weight loss days to be stressful. Whether you decide on a three-day apple vinegar diet, a seven-day diet or a four-week diet, optimal coordination of your day is necessary to ensure success.

Suggestions for Everyday Recipes

To be able to employ apple vinegar in weight loss on a daily basis, the diets should fit in the time periods between work and free time, between school and family, between business trips and home; in other words, it should adapt to your individual lifestyle. Therefore, you will be introduced to three suggestions for diets that vary in duration:

- the three-day apple vinegar diet;
- the seven-day apple vinegar diet;
- the four-week apple vinegar diet;

according to how much time you can and want to invest in your personal apple vinegar project. Here you can find the detailed suggestions for recipes for the entire day, from breakfast, to lunch, to dinner. The popular meals in between were also taken into consideration.

What Is Apple Vinegar?

Nutrients in the Apple

When apples ripen on a tree and they turn thick, round, red and yellow, many nutrients collect inside them.

- Pectin and numerous other fibers that give the apple its firmness.
- Vitamin C and bioflavonoids, that protect the fruit flesh and the seeds.
- Amino acids are in the peel of the apple to also protect the fruit flesh.
- The fruit flesh of the apple contains numerous depots, especially for:

  - Protein
  - Carbohydrates
  - Minerals
  - Water

Protecting Important Genetic Information...

The multitude of nutrients fulfills exclusively one purpose - to protect and to provide the seed with nutrition when the apple lies on the ground or in a pasture.

Ripe apples are not just sweet and fruity. They also contain a multitude of nutrients: Vitamin C, minerals and fibers, proteins, and carbohydrates. Apples are true "Biological Bombs".

Through the Immune System...

Only the seeds or sprouts are important to nature, because they guarantee the survival of the species. The same can be observed in other carriers of genetic information, such as eggs or roe. The species-endorsing genes are always protected against germs and other enemies through the immune system. At the same time, these genes are furnished with a large depot of all the important nutrients.

Acetic Acid - A Gift From Nature

- Like citric acid in fruits, or ascorbic acid (vitamin C) in fruit and vegetables, the acetic acid is also a mild organic acid and therefore, is easy on the stomach.
- Acetic acid destroys bacteria, viruses, fungi, parasites, and other microorganisms in rotting fruits - all of them pathogens. This is how the acetic acid protects genetic information.
- Acetic acid repels insects from overripe fruits by making the fruit flesh sour and inedible.
- Acetic acid is the enemy of all bacteria. Therefore, it also battles them inside the human stomach and intestines.
- Acetic acid has a disinfecting and detoxicating effect, even after it reaches the kidneys, the bladder, and the ureter.

Animals eat rotting fruit because they instinctively utilize the disinfecting effect of acetic acid. This acid is mild and easy on the stomach, and it detoxicates the body and frees it from pathogens.

Acetic Acid to Stay Healthy

Whenever animals get infected or poisoned, they instinctively seek rotting fruit. They wait as long as it takes for the alcohol to turn into acetic acid by way of fermentation. Only then do they eat the sour and rotting fruit to cleanse themselves from bacteria or other pathogens. This behavior can also be observed when the metabolism of the animal's organism threatens to collapse.

Detoxication Through Acetic Acid

Acetic acid cleanses the organism with its antibacterial effect. This is especially powerful in the area of the stomach and intestines - in other words, in the digestive system. Additionally, acetic acid also has a strong purifying effect on the inner organs, such as kidneys, bladder, and ureter, by aiding them in their function to detoxicate the body. Acetic acid also rebalances the metabolism of the body.

Naturally Slim With Apple Vinegar

How Vinegar Stops the Buildup of Fat

The acid contained in apple vinegar connects five lipolytic (fat-freeing) mechanisms. This guarantees the quick reduction of fat in the body. The process starts in the oral mucous tissue where the acetic acid blocks the hormonal signifiers and determines, within minutes, if an obese person chews something sweet, or other food containing carbohydrates (e.g., bread, noodles). This "one-way-street" travels from the intestines via blood and liver to the fat tissue. This activates enzymes in the smaller blood vessels that make fat by enclosing the fat cell. It is at this critical point that the introduction of triglycerides into the fat depots of the subcutis, or the fat of the hips or stomach, occurs in an obese person.

Vinegar for Stomach and Intestines

- Acetic acid locks acid in the stomach: It reduces the pH level and makes the stomach liquid acid. The adding of acid is important for the digestion of protein because only certain proteins, such as the stress hormones, contain the "golden key" to the opening of the adipozytes (fat cells).

- Acetic acid stimulates intestinal activity: It increases the transportation time of food. Therefore, only a certain percentage of the fat is digested and excreted - it does not reach the blood or the fat cells.

Their desire to consume sweets and foods containing salt makes it difficult for many people to lose weight. Apple vinegar does not just aid the body with the fat-reducing processes in the stomach and intestines, but also reduces the fateful craving for these fattening foods.

Desire for New Tastes

Vinegar entices your sense for new, unknown tastes by decreasing the craving for sweets and foods containing salt and fat, the worst enemy of your battle against the pounds.

Increase Cell Respiration

Acetic acid increases the respiratory function of the cell, and therefore increases the gain of energy and power of all cells. This process happens in two ways:

- Acetic acid highly improves the utilization of iron. Therefore, acetic acid enhances the production of red blood cells which carry oxygen to the body cells.
- Acetic acid increases the production of protein molecules in all cells. This leads to an increase in the metabolic rate, and one feels physically and mentally more vital.

Both effects of the acetic acid need body fat that has to be burned to create energy. This fat is withdrawn from the fat cells, therefore, one loses weight.

Acetic acid increases the respiratory function of the cell, stimulates the metabolism, and supports overall health. In both cases, the body's energy provider, fat, is burned.

Self-Test: Should You Use Apple Vinegar To Lose Weight?

Answer the following questions:	Yes	No

Are you more than 17 pounds (8 kilograms) overweight?

Are you oftentimes tired in the morning or the afternoon? *yes*

Is your excess weight mostly located in the stomach and hip area, but not so much in the subcutis (e.g., chest, arms, etc.)? *yes*

Is your stomach tighter and flatter in the morning than the evening? *yes*

Do you eat sweets at least twice daily?

Do you oftentimes suffer from diarrhea, gas, and odorous stools?

Are you oftentimes hungry at night?

Do you use a lot of salt on your food? *yes*

Are you oftentimes cold, even though you are dressed normally? *yes*

Has there been a time when your body was nice and slim? *yes*

Does it sometimes happen that you suddenly ("overnight", in other words, from one day to another) gain one or more kilograms (one to two pounds)?

Results:

One to two "yeses": The acid of the apple vinegar can help you only in the long run.

Three to eight "yeses": You are the ideal type for the apple vinegar diet. 6

Nine to ten "yeses": Your fat metabolism has several problems; you will need to use the apple vinegar diet for a longer period of time.

Right Before Going to Bed

- Make a good night snack from 1/2 avocado, 1 tsp. lemon juice, and pepper. Mash avocado with a fork; add a little lemon juice and pepper--done!

Beverages

You can drink vegetable juice, carbonated water, herbal tea, coffee, or black tea all day long. Please avoid sugar, but you can have sugar substitutes. All sweet drinks, such as lemonade or soda, are strictly forbidden. Also, stay away from sweet fruit juices containing a lot of fructose (fruit sugar); especially if you are a person who is predisposed to gain weight.

Decrease Fat Instead of Losing Water

Now you are done with this day's assignment and you can go to bed. Tomorrow morning you will get back on the scale. If you lost more than 1/2 pound (250 grams) in the course of one day, then you have reached your goal.

An important fact is that you do not just lose water with the apple vinegar combination diet (with exercise and meditation),

Maybe you are familiar with this phenomenon: only a few days after you finish a diet you followed strictly, you are back to your old weight. The reason is easily found - traditional weight loss diets cause you almost exclusively to lose water, but you need to burn fat to lose weight permanently.

as is often the case with other diets. The method introduced here is different in that the metabolism demands fat molecules so it can burn them. These are released from the fat areas of the stomach and hips, and are sent up to the body cells with the blood to be burned.

All other diets, though, keep the adipozites (fat cells) locked. Stingily, they release as little of the triglycerides (fat molecules) as possible. The consequence: The body takes the necessary fueling substances from the connective tissue (that causes wrinkles) and muscles (that causes you to feel listless and weak). The lost weight is almost exclusively water.

The best slimness acids are:
- *Acetic acid*
- *Citric acid*
- *Ascorbic acid*

Organic acids can be found in the entire body, but concentrated in the:
- *Stomach*
- *Intestines*
- *Blood*

These slimness acids fulfill a central and specific role in each single cell.

The most important task the organic acids perform are:
- *Stimulation of the immune system*
- *Strengthening of enzyme production*
- *Killing of bacteria*
- *Stimulation of cell reproduction*
- *Increase of cell energy*

Sour does not just make happy [German proverb], but it also makes slim: Use other organic acids in your nutrition besides acetic acid, e.g., citric acid and ascorbic acid (vitamin C).

You can let these organic acids - the slimness acids - work for you if you eat right and healthy. Take the eating habits of people in the Mediterranean as an example. You cannot just have a great vacation in those regions, you can also eat healthy. Add to those some healthy eating habits of your own.

- **Fish with lemon**

In southern regions of the Mediterranean, people have always added a few drops of lemon to their fish. The vitamin C of the lemon increases the digestibility of the fish substantially.

- **Salad with vinegar**

Another Mediterranean concoction is salad with sheep cheese, and a marinade containing vinegar. This use of vinegar enhances not only the taste, but also your health. The rules for these healthy and slim recipes have been handed down from generation to generation.

- **The health-promoting effect of vinegar**

Contrary to traditional weight loss diets that causes you mainly to lose water, the vinegar releases excess fat through the metabolism. This fat, necessary for the production of energy, is taken from the fat areas of your body - and you lose weight just in the right spots. Vinegar has another advantage: The lost fat from the adipozytes (fat cells) is not immediately replaced.

The Apple Vinegar Test Diet

Do excess pounds disappear with apple vinegar or not? To find out, here is a little test diet. When you have completed this apple vinegar test diet, then nothing should be between you and your dream figure for next summer's vacation.

The One-Day Test

- The apple vinegar test diet takes only one day. Start by weighing yourself in the morning.
- You can eat 2400 calories that day - and this is more than 90% of the total calories allowed by most all other weight loss programs. You won't be hungry.
- The apple vinegar diet is real tasty, and it will make you want to go through with the three-day diet, the seven-day diet, and the four-week diet. This guide will introduce you to all of these diets in greater detail.
- Two important activities support this apple vinegar diet:
    - A small exercise program
    - A simple meditation program

Cheating Only Helps the Pounds

Prerequisite for success: no cheating. Strictly follow the daily plan. If you don't muster the necessary strength, then you cheat yourself. Any deviations are strictly forbidden, and they only help you to retain those pounds, but if you follow the diet, then you are already closer to your dream body.

You can test your personal success with the apple vinegar diet in just one day, but to reach your goal "dream body" you will have to be more persistent.

Exercise - "The Big L"

This exercise improves your mood for the entire day:

- Lie down on your back
- Put hands under your head and lift head slightly
- Put legs together and lift up (L-position)
- Bring legs back down and then up again
- Repeat this exercise for three minutes

The test day starts by weighing yourself, followed by a glass of water with apple vinegar and honey. A breakfast and some exercise will give you the energy you need to start the day.

Your Schedule

In the Morning

The most important thing is to get up in a good mood. Don't dwell on the day. Try consciously to be in a good mood. Reward yourself with something nice for getting up, such as your favorite breakfast, some really good fruit, or a little surprise. Then weigh yourself and read your exact weight.

Breakfast

- Start the morning with a drink: 1 glass of carbonated water, 1 tablespoon apple vinegar, 1 tablespoon honey; mix all and stir well, then drink.
- Now we get to the real breakfast, containing: 1 slice of whole grain bread, 1 tsp. butter, 1 slice roast beef, (for vegetarians: 1 tofu sausage from your whole food store), 1 kiwi, 1 oz. (30 g) sheep cheese, 1 tomato, 6 olives, 1 small pickle, coffee or tea (please, no sugar or cream), and 1 egg. Spread butter on bread, add cold beef or sliced tofu sausage, and eat together with other food.

The test day starts by weighing yourself, followed by a glass of water with apple vinegar and honey. A breakfast and some exercise will give you the energy you need to start the day.

Before Noon

- For snacks, eat 1/2 cup of cereal. Grind the grains yourself, e.g., wheat, rye, oats, barley, or buckwheat. If you don't have a grain grinder, then get whole grain cereal from your whole food store.
- Important: Soak the grain overnight. Add diced fruit to your cereal. Choose seasonal fruit, e.g., strawberry, apple, banana, pear, orange, etc. Treat yourself to some milk.

Noon

Again, have a glass of water with apple vinegar and honey (see breakfast). For a light lunch, you can eat:

- 2 ounces (60 grams) fish [vegetarians, 3.5 oz. (100 grams) smoked tofu]
- very little fat (butter or vegetable oil for browning)
- green vegetables, e.g., mangel, spinach, broccoli, green cabbage, or leek; steam lightly
- 3 medium-sized potatoes with peel (from your whole food store)

Healing Assimilation

During the mediation, the so-called assimilation is reached: heart rate and pulse are reduced, cell activity, production of adrenaline, and the thyroid gland are slowed down. But the stomach and intestinal

Snacks are allowed! A freshly prepared whole grain cereal with fruits is an ideal source for energy in the morning.

activities are stimulated. The consequences: The intestines provide all 70 trillion body cells with numerous important minerals. After meditation you will be relaxed, and filled with energy.

Afternoon

Mix a snack:

- 1 container of yogurt
- 1 tablespoon sunflower seeds

Try to relax for a little while after lunch. Here are some suggestions. You can also choose another form of meditation that you prefer:

- Go for a walk by yourself. Walk in a forest or park.
- Listen to the murmur of water.
- Observe the clouds in the sky.
- Watch the tips of trees sway in the wind.
- Listen to the birds sing.

After a stressful morning, try some meditation exercises - those held outside are the best. Lunch is better digested, and the body can restore itself with energy for the rest of the day.

In the Early Evening - The Three-Minute "Hinge"

- Lie down on your back
- Hook feet under something heavy, such as a cabinet or a couch
- Stretch arms out behind your head
- Lift upper body, bending at the hip
- Bring upper body slowly back down
- Repeat this exercise for three minutes

In the Evening

- Have a glass of carbonated water with apple vinegar and honey. For dinner, have something light, containing:
    - 4 slices toast or 6 slices French bread
    - 1 plate raw vegetables
    - 1 3/4 ounces (50 grams) crab or 50 grams chicken [vegetarians: 3.5 oz. (100 grams) tofu]

Gaining Weight - Losing Weight

Good Times, Bad Times

Losing and gaining weight are regulatory mechanisms of the body to deal with the changing supply of food. Getting fat is an age-old emergency program for bad times. When the body is supplied with a lot of food, then the fat cells store energy in the form of yellow fat. That causes them to swell more and more. It is the responsibility of fat cells to create fat depots so they are available to the metabolism in times of hunger.

Fat Cells Help Against Stress

The storing of fat is only one of the many responsibilities these highly specialized cells have. They do far more: During the daily ups and downs of stress and relaxation, they provide fuel for all animals, as well as humans. They provide "cellular fuel" during periods of activity. That enables the body to be able to feel stimulated, awake, concentrated, and able to handle stress. This obviously also means that the body needs more fuel to be able to provide those services. It is during this time that the fat cells are emptied. During the quiet period following this, they increase their intake of depot fuel.

The storing of energy in the fat cells is a necessary process. During times of stress and physical strain, fat reserves are set free to be burned. This is the only way for the body to cope with bad times.

Short and Long Periods of Strain

This is the way Mother Nature ensures that the cells never run out of necessary fuel, and that they are ready to face everyday activities. Mostly glucose, or carbohydrates, are burned during short-term activities, whereas fat from the fat zones is burned when the body is engaged in long-term activities.

How Fat Cells Function

- A slim person owns approximately 20 billion fat cells. A fat person, on the other hand, easily has 150 billion fat cells.
- Fat cells like to build in the tissue of the subcutis. Here the fat protects you from the cold, but with bad nutrition, the subcutis tissue becomes fat and loose. Not a pretty sight!
- Excess fat first collects in the notorious areas: stomach, hips, rear, and upper thighs.
- Fat cells normally weigh (with a slim person) approximately a half microgram (a one-half millionth gram), but they can swell up to a multiple factor of their original weight.

When children and teenagers eat a lot of sweets, pastries made from white flour, fatty and salty foods (e.g., hamburger or pizza), and also drink a lot of soda and lemonade; they produce fat cells a lot earlier than necessary.

Being overweight is oftentimes the consequence of bad eating habits during childhood: French fries, hamburger, and sweets cause excessive buildup of fat cells. Only a change toward healthy nutrition will remove those fat areas around the stomach and hips permanently.

The Predisposition to Gain Weight

- Slim teenagers carry different amounts of fat cells with them. These fat cells are still empty, and they are therefore, not visible. But wrong nutrition creates a predisposition for overweight. The disposition will not be observable until years later. As adults, a person's body will react according to the patterns learned during childhood.
- Especially dangerous are the so-called preadipozytes. These empty fat cells weigh only one-half milligram. Slim people have up to 60 billion preadipozytes. Healthy nutrition ensures that these cells remain empty. But with an unhealthy diet, these cells can swell up to 200 times their original size, and they create fat zones. Up to 200 pounds (100 kilograms) of stomach fat are possible!
- Those who want to reduce their body weight permanently should not put all their hopes on apple vinegar. A determined change of your basic nutrition to natural foods is essential.

These Foods Make You Fat

- Sweet drinks such as lemonade, soda, coffee, or those that are sweetened too strongly - with a certain predisposition, also sweet fruit or sweet fruit juices
- Pastries made with lightly colored flour, such as noodles, white or mixed bread

Being fat is not just a mental problem - it is also a strain on your health. A diet with apple vinegar can help you to feel vital and fit again.

- Polished (white) rice
- Sausage
- Fatty meats
- Salty-crispy skin of fried or grilled poultry
- Fatty sauces, dressings, dip, mayonnaise
- Fatty sweet cakes, torts, or baked goods, chocolates, or candy
- Sweets, such as pralines
- Ice cream, sweet creamy desserts, tiramisu, and sweet puddings
- All alcoholic beverages, such as schnapps, liquor, and sweet wines, but also beer, wine and liquor, if consumed in great quantities
- Too much cream or fat cheese

Foods That Make You Slim

- Fruit
- Salad
- Vegetables
- Raw vegetables
- Whole grain products
- Natural rice
- Potatoes
- Seafood
- Lean meat
- Soy or tofu products
- Curd cheese and low-fat yogurt
- Low-fat cheese

Mother Nature Wants Slim Creatures

A multitude of plants has developed over the past three to four million years. Much later, animals came along. Approximately 200,000 years ago, the first humans appeared. Mother Nature built a natural slimming program into animals, as well as humans. That means that only creatures of normal body weight are fit for survival, and are able to win the battle of existence in the greater scheme of evolution. For example: An animal in the wild who is only one percent overweight will already be hampered, or unable to survive. Exceptions are mothers, or animals that need depots of fat for the winter months (e.g., bears).

As mentioned before, the human also follows this slimming principle. In other words: In each obese person there exists, genetically speaking, a slim one. That slim person within just needs to be awakened. No other food helps more with this than apple vinegar, or other kinds of vinegar.

Secret Weapon-Growth Hormone

For millions of years, Mother Nature has helped all creatures to remain slim and fit for survival. The cause is a special growth hormone that prevents animals, as well as people, from becoming obese. At the same time, this hormone provides the organism with much vitality and energy.

Who would not like to lose a few pounds overnight? This dream can come true because the pituitary gland produces the growth hormone at night: This hormone acts as a natural slimmer-downer.

Control from the Brain

This growth hormone is produced from pure protein in the pituitary gland. The relatively large molecule is made of 189 amino acids (building blocks of protein) - other protein compounds sometimes contain only ten amino acids, or less.

The human pituitary glad is approximately the size of a cherry pit. It contains mostly water, the growth hormone, and some other hormones.

Slim With The Growth Hormone

- The pituitary gland starts its production of the growth hormone 70 minutes after going to sleep.
- The concentration of the growth hormone increases up to 40 times its normal value.
- The growth hormone is a stress hormone. That means that it is, contrary to other hormones, able to "unlock" the fat cells, or to set fat free.
- The growth hormone makes it possible for the fat molecules (triglycerides) to be dissolved, which in turn go to all body cells via the blood, but especially to the muscle cells.
- At night, these cells burn energy. With approximately 70 trillion body cells, this accumulates. You wake up slimmer - or a little lighter - and full of energy in the morning.

The fat-freeing effect of the growth hormone is best supported with a dinner rich in protein, and a good night drink that is unsweetened and rich in vitamin C (because sugar destroys vitamin C).

Helpful Vitamin C

If you find out in the morning, while weighing yourself, that you have lost weight (even a little) overnight, then this is due to the growth hormone, the most important slimmer-downer of Mother Nature. It is therefore, especially important to support the production of this lipolytic (fat freeing) hormone in the pituitary gland. It has been known since the mid-nineties that obese, heavy people produce little or no growth hormone. The reason: They don't have enough protein at their disposal. The pituitary gland also needs vitamin C for the biosynthesis of the growth hormone. Interestingly enough, this small gland has the highest concentration of vitamin C of all body parts.

Lose Weight in Your Sleep

The Ideal Dinner

Lose weight in your sleep - all but a dream. It works easily if you follow these steps:

- Have a dinner that is rich in protein, e.g., a big platter of raw vegetables with egg, tuna, chicken strips, lean ham, crab, cold lean beef, or (for vegetarians) two slices tofu sausage. You can have four slices of toast or French bread with this.
- Make dressing for raw vegetables with apple vinegar and olive oil.
- Drink a cup or 8 oz. (1 /4 liter) carbonated water with apple vinegar and honey (1 tablespoon each).
- Don't eat between dinner and bedtime. Only drink your own juice made with pressed lemon juice and carbonated water. Use at least two lemons. Don't sweeten this beverage; it should be consumed as tart as possible.

Apple vinegar drinks and raw vegetables enriched with vinegar are optimal for the ample production of the growth hormone. The acetic acid contained in the stomach and intestines dissolves the protein contained in meat and fish into amino acids: These are the "main dishes" of the pituitary gland.

Energy Push for Hormone Production

Everything else is up to your pituitary gland. The apple vinegar beverages, and the vinegar contained in the raw vegetables, will dissect the protein optimally with the help of the amino acids. By half an hour after dinner, a steady stream of protein building blocks is released from the intestines into the blood.

The pituitary gland is interspersed with a dense and small labyrinth of the finest blood vessels. The gland cells take the protein from these small blood vessels. At the same time, the blood is enormously filled with their favorite, vitamin C. Now they reach their full capacity, because now they have access to the most important basic raw materials for the production of their hormones.

Control Via the Light

As long as the sun is shining, and it is light, or there is at least a light source, the pituitary gland produces the day-active hormones that are important for our overall alert and concentrated being. The so-called gonaootrope hormones are also produced; they are responsible for sexual and reproductive functions. But if the light effects cease with the late hour, and we go to sleep, then the pituitary gland stops producing those day hormones; it now pumps the growth hormone into the blood.

The big hormone molecules eventually invade the entire blood vessels - each adult has approximately 62,000 miles (100,000 kilometers) of blood vessels!

- The growth hormone ensures that the fat cells are opened, and the fat set free, so that they circulate in the blood.

- The hormone also stimulates the growth function of the body; the mitosis (cell division), the growth of muscles or connective tissue, hair and fingernails, immune cells, or mucous tissue cells.

Mitochondria - Burners of Energy

Ample cell activity is necessary for growth. This means the amount of so-called mitochondria is increased in the cells. Mitochondria are little burners of energy where oxygen and burnable fat are collected. The more growth hormones pressed into the blood stream, the more fat you will burn - and the slimmer and more vital you wake up the next morning.

Growth Hormone and Acetic Acid

The growth hormone, this nocturnal slimmer provided by Mother Nature, requires a companion - acetic acid. You probably noticed: Whenever you wake up suddenly at night, you have a sour taste in your mouth. This is caused by saliva and gastric acid that are enriched with more acid to digest the protein contained in food. This process can be further enhanced with a glass of apple vinegar. This will get the fat-melting process going - and 80 trillion body cells burn fat like they were meant to.

Healthy Food With Apple Vinegar

Lust for Food Makes Fat

The biggest dilemma many obese people encounter is the craving for two kinds of food:

- The addiction for sweets
- The lust for food containing lots of fat and salt.

The Addiction for Sweets

The craving for something sweet oftentimes finds its origin in a low blood sugar level (glucose level). Whenever the glucose level, or blood sugar level decreases, a person feels the urgent need to eat chocolates, pralines, candy bars, sweet cookies, foods containing cream, candy, or other sweets. This craving is initiated by the brain, and can be so irresistible that the person in question cannot appreciate the many finer taste variations, such as vegetables.

Our eating habits are formed in early childhood. It is very hard to change one's appetite from fatty, salty foods to tasty and healthy dishes based on vegetables, mushrooms, or whole grain products.

The Craving for Fat and Salt

Many people are wild about foods containing a lot of fat and salt: hot dogs with french fries, turkey with a fatty, salty crust, fat sauces, hamburger, pizza, liver, sausage, pepperoni, white sauces, chicken soups, salty meats, etc.

Fat alone does not have any taste. The protein (e.g., in fried foods or steak) is also neutral in taste. It is only the salt and spices that make these dishes favorites on our menus. The same holds true for all canned foods, and ready-to-eat frozen dishes.

The Dilemma With the Blood Sugar Level

- The blood sugar level is especially important for the brain and nerves, for they accept only pure glucose as fuel. On the other hand, other cells, such as muscle cells, can burn other substances, such as fat.
- Brain and nerve cells can only function properly if the glucose values are in the area of 90 milligrams of glucose to 100 milligrams of blood.

Sinking Glucose Levels

- When the level decreases to 65 milligrams of glucose to 100 milligrams of blood, one gets nervous and irritated.
- When the glucose level drops to 55 milligrams of glucose to 100 milligrams of blood, a person tires quickly and tries to avoid conflict.
- At a level of 45 milligrams of glucose to 100 milligrams of

blood, it becomes hard to concentrate, and one has the desire to hide. Soon, depressive moods set in.

- If a person resorts to consuming sweets (or alcohol), then the carbohydrates contained in them are quickly dissolved into the blood and are sent to the brain and nerve cells. The blood sugar level increases, and a person feels better quickly.
- This feeling of well being does not last very long, though: After only 20 minutes, the glucose level sinks again - and oftentimes plunges below the previous low level.

Apple Vinegar Can Help

Apple vinegar regulates the ups and downs of the glucose level.

- Vinegar opens the taste sensors for food, increasing the blood sugar level, e.g., vegetables, fruit, or whole grain products.

- Vinegar makes protein easily digestible, and a good digestion of protein is a prerequisite to feeling mentally and physically fit.

Many people complain about nervosity, tiredness, and the lack of ability to concentrate at work, at school, or during their free time. These are oftentimes symptoms of a low blood sugar level. Chocolates, or glucose, are only fixes in the short run. Vinegar on the other hand, creates cravings for vegetables, fruits, and whole grain products that increase the sugar level in the long run.

Salt as a Mentor of Fat

Do you really want to get rid of fat around your stomach and hips? Then ban salt from your meal plan as much as possible, and substitute it with other spices. Besides pepper, paprika, curry, spices, or other fresh herbs, taste enhancers containing vinegar, such as:

- apple vinegar
- catsup containing vinegar
- mustard containing vinegar
- marinades, mayonnaise, dressings, dip based on vinegar

lend themselves to this.

Here are some food suggestions ideal to steer your meal plan away from salt, and lead it towards other taste explorations:

- vegetables marinated in vinegar
- mushrooms marinated in vinegar
- mixed pickles

Vinegar in Your Meal Plan

Try to slowly substitute salt with vinegar. You will soon learn to love and enjoy the new taste: Food can taste great without salt.

- Eat a plate of raw vegetables, or a salad, at least once daily. Dress the salad with high-quality vegetable oil. Soy oil, sunflower seed oil, and olive oil are excellent choices. The part of unsaturated fatty acids in the oil should be high. Also, use vinegar, or better, use apple vinegar for your salad dressing.

Strong spices add a great, spiffy taste to most dishes, but you should avoid salt, or substitute it with herbs, or taste enhancers containing vinegar. A salad made with fresh herbs, apple vinegar, and oil also tastes good without salt.

- Apple vinegar is also a healthy substitute to use as a spice for sour kidneys or liver, for sauces, and for cheese.
- Many kinds of vegetables can be improved by adding a few drops of vinegar. That is the first step to be able to enjoy the unique tastes of fine vegetables, and one day you will be able to enjoy them without vinegar.

The Quantity is Important

The pectin fibers, vitamins or minerals contained in vinegar, are valuable to the human metabolism. Even though their concentration is small compared to others, by far more important is the acetic acid that controls the production of more gastric acid, which provides the cells with fresh protein, calcium, and iron. The vinegar also stimulates the intestinal activity, removes digestive problems, and removes useless fat from the body via the stools, preventing it from turning into permanent fat.

Nonetheless, vinegar should be used sparingly in the kitchen, by the drop, teaspoon, or at the most, tablespoon. This is also true for beverages with vinegar, It does not make sense to consume too much vinegar – you will not lose weight faster that way.

You can add apple vinegar and other kinds of vinegar to your meal plan in many ways, but do not make the mistake of thinking, "more is better". Vinegar should only be added to beverages and meals by the drop or teaspoon.

Little Salt for a Slim Body

- *Salt is necessary for the body - but only in small quantities.*

- *Cooking salt is made of sodium chloride [NaCl]. The sodium transports nutrients from the intestines into the blood. Therefore, the intestinal walls, with their crowded system of blood vessels, contain a lot of sodium.*

- *Sodium can be fatal for the figure in that it causes the body to retain great amounts of water. The more salt you consume, the more water collects in the stomach area. Some people carry up to five pounds of excess weight in water .*

- *Even very active athletes cannot lose their gut if they eat too much salt.*

- *Sodium binds water in the blood. This increases blood volume, and the blood pressure with it.*

- *Another negative effect of sodium: It increases the tormus, the tension of the vessel walls inside the veins. This makes the vessels smaller, and increases the blood pressure again.*

- *The substitution of vinegar for salt can quickly make or break your weight loss diet.*

The Eight-Day Test

Modern biochemists and metabolism experts give all obese people the following advice: Switch from salt to vinegar. Substitute where possible. Substitute vinegar, herbs, and spices for salt. Just try - with this easy eight-day test:

The first day:
Weigh yourself the first day and write down your actual weight.

- Fill half of a really small container with salt. This amount has to last for the entire week.
- Besides spices, herbs, garlic, and onions, you should use vinegar exclusively to enhance taste.

The second day:
Your taste buds are slowly adjusting to the change. They learn to enjoy meals without a lot of salt.

The third and fourth day:
No later than the fourth day, you will discover your preference for foods you rarely ate up until then, such as celery, carrots, asparagus, fennel, cabbage, leek, mangel, beans, lentils, or peas. Give in to your new cravings, and also try some new recipes.

The fifth and sixth day:
If you haven't already, you will find out no later than the sixth day: You can live without meat or poultry or, in other words, all those foods that contain a lot of salt.

Our taste buds are, unfortunately, too used to salty foods. Salt has the negative quality to bind water in tissue. That is why salt causes us to gain weight. Also, your blood pressure will thank you for switching to vinegar.

The seventh day:

You may have already discovered that by the seventh day, the acetic vinegar has helped you to develop a new attitude toward cooking and eating. Vegetables, beans and peas, mushrooms, potatoes, and natural rice - all these foods now develop their own unique taste. A whole new world of a healthy way to eat has been opened up for your taste buds.

The eighth day:

You will experience the greatest joy when you step on the scale on the morning of the eighth day. Now the pounds are gone, and not just because you lost water, but you also lost a lot of fat. You graduated from the eight-day test with honors.

Detoxicate the Intestines

Losing weight by means of healthy nutrition is a process involving all functions of the body. From the mouth, via the stomach and intestines - all digestive organs are involved. The effective diet starts in the mouth where now, hopefully, slim foods are being chewed carefully. The stomach predigests the protein, which has a very slimming effect. The third, and most important site, are the intestines. A well-functioning intestine is a necessary prerequisite for a perfect metabolism that reduces the stomach and hips.

A prerequisite for a healthy metabolism is an intact intestinal environment. Poor nutrition causes the increase of bacteria and fungi and can lead to damage of the intestinal mucous tissue. Unpleasant constipation, gas, or diarrhea are the consequences of these pathogens. Apple vinegar helps you fight these problems.

44

The Wonderland of Digestion

A very healthy intestinal mucous membrane looks like a luscious tropical jungle under the microscope: Everywhere there is a thick growth of villi and outgrowth, grooves and faults. This gives the mucous membrane an enormous amount of surface. If one could lay the human intestines out entirely, it would be as big as a tennis court.

The food mash of each meal covers the mucous membrane like a very thin film. This enables the intestines to transfer each nutritious molecule to the blood.

In cases of malnutrition, or attacks of bacteria or fungi, the surface structure of the intestines becomes thinner and smaller. The mucous membrane wastes away; it can even cause callus-like places to form. The intestines lose their important function to protect you from germs as part of the immune system. The constant intestinal activities occur only at a snail's pace. More and more poisons and damaging microorganisms build up, and the necessary intestinal flora in the colon breaks partially down. If it has not already, the fat metabolism will become imbalanced inside the intestines: The levels of cholesterol and lipids increase in the blood. Additionally, more and more triglycerides (fat molecules) rush to get to the already enlarged fat cells.

Gastric acid destroys bacteria before it reaches the intestines. The acetic acid in food enhances the acid bath in the stomach.

The Sour Barrier in Your Stomach

Apple vinegar clears the road to a slimmer body because it cleans out all the numerous bacteria that hinder the process of digestion. Because viruses cannot handle warmth or heat very well, they become extinct when exposed to fever. Bacteria, first and foremost, show an "allergic reaction" to acids.

Bacteria need the basic alkaline and mild environment of the digestive juices of the intestines; that is why they love to settle in the intestines to build their huge colonies.

To get to the stomach, the bacteria first have to get through the stomach - that barrier where the gastric acid destroys a majority of the bacteria. Apple vinegar will enhance the acid environment of your stomach and build a barrier for bacteria as it travels to the intestines.

Protection From Pathogens

Some people wash their salad five times, and then look at each individual leaf; "Now it is really clean, no trace of any microorganisms".

The reality of food looks different: No matter how carefully you wash and scrub, and rinse and scratch, any food, e.g., salad leaves, will always show a flowering world of hundreds of different pathogens when viewed under the microscope: Fungi, parasites, viruses, bacteria, and other microbiological life forms. To protect the body from those dangers, Mother Nature invented gastric acid.

Medicine for the Stomach

Germs, such as bacteroids or clostridium germs, are especially damaging for the sensitive mucous tissue of the small intestine because they can disturb the burning of fat cells. These tiny villains eat valuable vitamins, and turn the usually hapless reduction of carbohydrates inside the intestines into a big problem. The consequence: Fatty stool, vitamin deficiency, diarrhea, gas, and colic. Apple vinegar is a natural medicine from Mother Nature's pharmacy that prevents such ailments - and practically with no effort. The intake of apple vinegar alone initiates the following protective processes:

- The pH level of the stomach sinks, the amount of acid inside the stomach increases, and it destroys all bacteria contained in the food within seconds. Now these bacteria cannot enter and settle in the smaller intestines.

Intestinal Peristalsis

Through the wave-like contractions of the intestines that move the food mash forward, poisons and harmful substances, viruses, fungi, and bacteria are excreted via the stool. The following problem oftentimes occurs: Those who eat mostly sweets, pastries made from lightly colored flour, and salty-fatty products, will hardly have any digestive activity left. The consequence is that the colonies of pathogens in the small intestines are now nearly undisturbed, and the settlement of fungi and bacteria becomes too numerous.

Sweet and fatty foods don't just make the intestines lazy, but they are also a breeding ground for fungi and other pathogens. A healthy diet simply causes those parasites to starve to death.

When the Gall Acid is Missing

Another damaging side effect of bacteria infestation is the decrease of the important gall acid. The consequences are far-reaching, and can even cause life-threatening diseases:

- Free gall acids destroy the intestinal tissue.
- Little vitamin B_{12} (necessary to produce blood, to work muscles, and to be mentally fit) is transferred to the blood.
- The breakdown of protein into amino acids is slowed down, therefore causing the protein levels of the blood to decrease rapidly.
- The originally healthy intestinal environment of the colon changes its character. Dangerous pathogens reign here as well, leading to constipation and poisoning, and in the worst case, even to colon cancer.

Stomach intestines must therefore be disinfected daily. They must be detoxified, and kept free from bacteria and other pathogens. Nothing helps better than acetic acid. In the long term, one drink containing apple vinegar before, with, or after every meal will provide you with a healthy intestinal environment.

Gas, stomachaches, constipation, and diarrhea are symptoms of intestinal problems. If you consume apple vinegar regularly, these ailments will disappear because the vinegar destroys the bacteria in the intestines and enhances the production of digestive enzymes. A side effect on the slim side:
Apple vinegar reduces hunger.

Prevent Infectious Intestinal Diseases

Infectious diseases such as Colitis Ulcerose or Morbus Crohn, are typical diseases of our civilization. They are closely related to unhealthy nutrition. The risk factors for infectious intestinal diseases are:

- Nutrition low in fiber
- Too much sugar
- Too much coffee consumption
- Stress

To prevent intestinal diseases, you have to change your eating and living habits:

- Consume as many fibers as possible with your diet, especially in the form of raw vegetables.
- Avoid white sugar as much as possible.
- If your stomach is sensitive and "nervous", then you should reduce your intake of coffee, for certain substances in the coffee are an additional stress on your intestinal environment. If that is hard for you to do, then you should at least try to switch to coffee that has been roasted in a way that will be less offensive to your stomach.
- Control your stress, and try especially to reduce stress-intensive periods with better organization.

An apple vinegar diet can strengthen the intestinal environment, and therefore create an important prerequisite to prevent intestinal diseases. Long-term changes for a healthy diet which includes a lot of fiber, e.g., raw vegetables, are helpful as well.

Genetic Causes for Overweight

Some people cannot lose weight, even though they only consume coffee, chewing gum, and a few cookies. The reason is that the triglycerides hold on to the fat cells and won't leave their "home" at any price. Supposedly, nobody can help in this situation - no doctor and no weight loss diet. But it is relatively easy for these people to lose weight. Unfortunately, it is not enough to just drink apple vinegar. One important prerequisite for success is to know the reasons for being overweight.

Being Fat - Genetic Reasons?

Slimness and Obesity Genes

Everything that happens inside the body is ordered by the genes that sit in the nucleus of a cell. Protein executes these orders. All other nutrients, such as vitamins, minerals, fatty acids, or glucose, are merely helpers in this process. There are genes in charge of the growth of hair, or the production of the happy hormone, as well as genes responsible for muscle growth. There are genes that order the fat cells to expel their excess fat so the body can burn it to create energy. But there are also the so-called obesity-genes that keep the fat in the fat cells. These obesity genes slowly gain the upper hand over the slimness genes if a person eats poorly for years.

Genes greatly influence body weight: The obesity genes keep the fat in the fat cells. In cases of long-term poor nutrition, these obesity genes dominate those promoting health and weight loss.

Mutations Lead to Fat Depots

The triggers for gene mutations are certain adeno viruses that live off fat and are interested in fat cells full of yellow fat.

These mutations from slimness to obesity genes have to be reversed. The obesity genes that have been dominant until now have to lose their importance as quickly as possible. Dominating and reactivating the slimness genes as Mother Nature intended can only do this. When this is accomplished, the "one-way-street fat" is reversed. It no longer takes the route through the intestines via the blood and liver to the fat areas, but reverses from the fat depots via the blood to the muscle cells and other body cells. Depending on the degree of obesity, this can create relevant weight loss in a short period of time.

Fight Fat With Apple Vinegar

Apple vinegar can play an important and stimulating role in reversing the development of more and more fat:

- Before each meal, always drink 1 glass of carbonated water, or water from the faucet, mixed with 1 tablespoon apple vinegar. Important: Please do not add any honey or other sweeteners.
- In the morning, the afternoon, and late at night, you should also drink a glass of water with apple vinegar.

The centerpiece of the apple vinegar diet is the glass of water containing apple vinegar before each meal, but you should also drink this beverage between meals, unsweetened.

Eat as Much as You Want

With the right nutrition and foods allowed, quantity is unlimited. Therefore, you do not need to count calories. You can eat as much of those foods as you wish. Even 4,000 calories a day can make you slimmer, rather than fatter.

Foods You Are Allowed to Eat

By consuming only the following foods, even very obese people can easily lose weight:

- Whole grain breads, pumpernickel, toast
- Low-fat cheese, curd cheese, yogurt
- All slightly or really tart kinds of fruit, such as apples, sour cherries, blueberries, raspberries, cranberries, gooseberries, grapefruits, lemons, kiwi, oranges
- All vegetables (raw or slightly steamed), mushrooms
- Potatoes, natural rice, whole wheat noodles
- Crab, cold water fish (portions no bigger than 60 grams)
- Roast beef, low-fat ham
- Chicken (skinless)
- Soy and tofu products
- Butter, vegetable oil
- Whole grain cereal from rye, wheat, oats, barley, buckwheat, millet
- Use apple vinegar, garlic, onions, horseradish, mustard, pepper, paprika, and curry for spices, and very little salt.

The most important factor of any weight loss diet is the change to healthy nutrition: fruits, vegetables, whole wheat products, lean meat and fish. These are all healthy and can be used in numerous tasty recipes.

Beverages You Are Allowed to Have

- During the first week you can drink these beverages: coffee, black or green tea, herbal tea without sugar or cream (artificial sweeteners are allowed), vegetable juices, tomato juice or tart fruit juices, carbonated water or water from the faucet, as well as buttermilk.
- Starting with week two, you can also have sweeter fruit juices such as apple juice, orange juice, as well as half a liter of beer, or a quarter liter of wine, daily.

Changes in the Fat Metabolism

By the second day, with a little apple vinegar, such a diet will cause immense differences in the metabolism of the fat cells:

- The concentration of fat-producing adeno viruses increases.
- The number of fattening enzymes in transit between blood vessels and fat cells is reduced.
- The fat cells open under the influence of the stress hormone and give their content to the blood, changing into energy in the body cells.
- You already feel fresher and more vital in the morning, and you clearly lose weight.

Many beverages also make fat, but allowed are unsweetened tea and coffee, water, vegetable juices, and tart fruit juices. Wait for that little taste of beer or wine until you graduate into the second week of the program.

Healthy Exercises

This apple vinegar diet must be supported with exercise. The following rules apply:

- During the first two days of the diet, you should exercise as much as possible.
- This newly acquired status of exercise should be doubled on the third day.
- Thereafter, add an additional two units of intensive training. Each unit lasts three minutes.

This can be done in the morning, during your lunch break, or in the evening; it will only take a few minutes. Give yourself a push and exercise.

You can easily incorporate the following three exercises into your daily schedule:

You should be willing to invest in a little exercise for your dream body. Short gymnastic exercises for rear and stomach can fit into any schedule, even though it may be crowded.

"Torture Muscles"

- Lie down on your back
- Bring legs up, bending at the knees
- Place hands behind and under the head
- Lift upper body as far as possible from floor
- Hold for approximately one minute (or as long as you can)
- After that, relax for a short time (but no longer than 10 seconds)

"Stomach Swimming"

- Lie down on stomach
- Lift upper body as far as possible off the floor
- Stretch arms to front, and then pull back to your rear
- Repeat this exercise, lifting one leg and then the other
- Finally, imitate the movements of swimming with your legs lifted off the floor

"Knee Swing"

- Bend down, put weight on heels, and balance with hands behind your back
- Lift rear and arms with your back stiff
- Repeat this exercise for one minute
- Put weight again on heels and arms, lift pelvis and remain in position for a minute (if possible)
- Lift rear and arms a few centimeters from the heels and remain in this position

The more you perspire, the more weight you lose. When engaged in endurance exercises, such as jogging, riding a bicycle, or aerobics, the body does not just burn carbohydrates, but also much fat, but be careful: The unfit should not overdo it.

From Lipogenesis to Lipolysis

Any other stretching or yoga exercise fulfills the same purpose. All perspiration-producing forms of exercise support the change from the fattening lipogenesis (fat increase) to the slimming lipolysis (fat decrease). This especially includes jazz dancing, aerobics, fast stair-climbing, and also push-ups. Ideal would also be jogging, walking, fast and active walking or hiking, riding a bicycle, or hiking in the mountains.

Cold Makes Slim

- Don't put on too many clothes for your exercising, but rather choose something light. Body heat is best and healthiest when produced through your own movement.
- Walking - or other sports – done in the rain or snow, stimulate the fat-freeing genes even more.
- Scientists seriously recommend: Go ahead and get wet if it rains. Then go home and take a shower and rub yourself dry with a towel.
- Don't use heavy, warm, blankets at night. They should be light, but comfortable enough so you do not freeze.
- Do not overheat your home.

The More Exercise, the Better

Each sport activity enhances the rate of metabolism of the body. The muscle cells demand more depot fat to be burned. Proteins in the fat areas are activated so that numerous triglycerides are transferred to the blood. With an intensive apple vinegar diet, chosen foods, and exercise, your fat cells won't have a choice: Under the leadership of the impartial slimness genes, they shrivel and the body weight decreases rapidly.

Three-Day Apple Vinegar Diet

A Quick Diet for the Impatient

Don't expect a great weight loss from this quick diet, but you will still lose some pounds. The great loss of water due to potassium ensures that:

- Three quarters of the lost weight is water.
- Only one quarter of the lost weight is fat.
- The water loss is substantial and, depending on body volume, much higher than with normal weight loss diets.
- Glucose is responsible for one-half of the water loss, because it is burned to gain energy. Each gram of depot glucose is bound to 2.7 grams of water, which is also lost when the glucose is burned.

Foods with a High Content of Potassium

Potassium and sodium are the central opponents in human water management: sodium (in cooking salt) sucks water into the blood and binds it inside the body. Potassium, on the other hand, dehydrates, meaning it transports the water to the kidneys so it can be excreted.

An especially high content of potassium can be found in avocados, green vegetables, cabbage, peas and beans, celery, potatoes, asparagus, salad, bananas, whole wheat products, and milk. Therefore,

A good start to the day is best accomplished with a healthy breakfast. Vary the ingredients mentioned above to go with your favorite breakfast.

these products play a key role in the three-day apple vinegar diet.

This quick weight loss diet is effectively supported by three-minute exercises, so your body moves and perspires. Other small activities are also beneficial.

What You Can Eat

In the following, you will find some suggestions for recipes:
Choose according to your preference and appetite:

- You can drink coffee, black or green tea, herbal tea, or warm milk (please do not use any sugar, but you can use fat-reduced cream and sugar substitutes).
- Before breakfast, drink a small glass, 1 cup (0.2 liters) of water, to which you have added 1 tablespoon apple vinegar.

Losing Weight According to Table:
With the three-day diet you will lose a total weight of (water and fat):

Overweight	Water & Fat Together
• 67 lbs (30kg)	approx. 7 pounds (3100g)
• 45 lbs (20kg)	approx. 6 pounds (2600g)
• 22 lbs (10kg)	approx. 3.75 pounds (1700g)
• 11 lbs (5kg)	approx. 2.5 pounds (1100g)

Potassium helps with the dehydration of the body. Green vegetables, avocados, bananas, and other foods containing high percentages of potassium are, therefore, of great importance in this diet.

Breakfast

Prosciutto -Pickle Sandwich

Ingredients: 1 slice of whole grain bread, 1 tsp. butter, 1 slice of lean prosciutto, 1 small pickle, low-fat mayonnaise, salt, pepper.
Preparation: Spread butter on whole grain bread, put prosciutto on top, slice pickle, put on top of prosciutto. Dress with low-fat mayonnaise, sprinkle with salt and pepper.

Turkish Breakfast

Ingredients: 1 egg, 1 firm tomato, 1 oz. (30 g) of cucumber, 1 3/4 oz. (50 g) sheep cheese, 5 olives, 3 slices of toast, salt, pepper.
Preparation: Boil egg until hard and slice; peel tomato and dice; slice cucumber. Dice sheep cheese and put everything on toast. Spice to taste with salt and pepper.

Fruit Breakfast

Ingredients: 1 banana, 1 kiwi, 1 apple, 1 cup of yogurt, 1 tablespoon of sunflower seeds.
Preparation: Chop banana, kiwi, and apple; mix with yogurt; sprinkle sunflower seeds on top.

Pumpernickel with Curd Cheese

Ingredients: 4 tablespoons low-fat curd cheese, 1 tsp. sour cream, herbal salt, pepper, paprika, 1 tsp. chopped mixed herbs, 2 slices of pumpernickel.
Preparation: Mix curd cheese with low-fat sour cream; stir in spices and herbs; spread mixture on slices of bread.

Snacks

Drink a small glass of water, 1 cup (0.2 liters), with 1 tablespoon apple vinegar before each snack. Healthy snacks are:

- 1 tofu sausage with mustard and 1 slice of toast.
- 1 serving whole wheat cereal (1/2 cup) with chopped fruit mixed with yogurt.
- 1 slice of roast beef on 1 slice of toast; add a little bit of chopped pickles.
- 1 slice of pumpernickel spread with 1 tsp. butter; add 1/2 sliced egg, paprika, and salt.
- 1 slice of honeydew melon with 1 thin slice of prosciutto, and 1 slice of toast.
- 1 oz. (30 grams) of nonsulfated dried fruit (from your whole food store).
- 1 big rasped carrot dressed with a little vegetable oil and apple vinegar; spice to taste with salt and pepper. Also, 1 slice of whole grain bread.
- 1/2 avocado, mash with fork; add lemon juice, pepper, and a little salt.
- 1 oz. (30 grams) of soy snacks (from your whole food store).

Some like a hefty breakfast, others a fruity one. Whatever type you may be, after a healthy breakfast you can start your day full of energy, and in a good mood.

Lunch

- The main emphasis of lunch should be dehydrating vegetables and mushrooms, which you should steam only slightly in water. This ensures that all the important vitamins and minerals survive.
- The energy fuels are all provided with carbohydrates, which can be found in great quantities in natural rice, whole grain pastries, and potatoes.
- You should have only a little fat in the form of butter, or high-quality vegetable oil, so that the organs have to get as much fat as possible from the depots around the stomach, hips, rear, and upper thighs. That is the most important step toward success with the three-day apple vinegar diet.
- Complex carbohydrates (from whole grain products, vegetables, etc.) and a little protein from meat, fish, poultry, or tofu, increase the blood sugar level. This ensures that you will not feel as tired and will be more stimulated: As the metabolism productivity increases, the lipolysis (fat-freeing process) reaches its optimum.

All of the following recipes are merely suggestions. Based on vegetables and mushrooms, as well as healthy whole grain products, you can create your own menu by using just a little imagination.

You will maintain a healthier body if you have many little snacks throughout the day. A fruit cereal for breakfast gives new strength and energy - and you won't be tired in the morning.

Turkey with Brussels Sprouts

Ingredients: 2 oz. (60 g) of turkey breast, 7 oz. (200 g) of Brussels sprouts, 1 diced onion, 1 tablespoon butter or lard, salt, pepper, 1 tablespoon vegetable oil, 1 tablespoon apple vinegar, 1 tablespoon roasted almond slivers.

Preparation: Clean turkey breast thoroughly and dice. Clean and wash Brussels sprouts and put in a pot with little water. Bring to boil, then simmer for 20 minutes, or until done. Drain in colander. Glaze onions in frying pan with butter or lard. Add diced turkey and fry until golden brown. Add salt and pepper and mix with vegetable oil and apple vinegar. Put on plate, cover with Brussels sprouts, and sprinkle almond slivers on top.

Mushroom-Cucumber Casserole

Ingredients: 4 tablespoons natural rice, 1 cucumber, 1 cup or 8 oz. (1/4 liter) vegetable broth, 1 diced onion, 1 tablespoon vegetable oil, 1 big tomato, 3.5 oz. (100 grams) mushrooms, salt, pepper, paprika, 1 tsp. chopped parsley, 1 tsp. marjoram, 2 tsp. ground Parmesan cheese.

Preparation: Boil rice al a dente. Wash and peel cucumber, cut in half, remove seeds with spoon and steam in vegetable broth for 5 minutes. Glaze onions in oil until golden brown. Peel tomato and dice; wash and cut mushrooms; put both in pan with onions. Add salt, pepper, and paprika. Sauté for 5 minutes. Add parsley and marjoram. Butter casserole dish, put cucumber halves on bottom and fill with tomato-mushroom filling. Cover with Parmesan cheese and bake in 420° F (200° C) oven for 12 minutes. Serve with natural rice.

Vegetables and mushrooms that enhance dehydrating should be the main ingredient of your lunch. Be inspired by the recipes suggested here, and experiment to create new variations.

Spicy Pork Filet

Ingredients: 3 potatoes, 5 oz. (150 g) pork filet, 1 tablespoon vegetable oil, 1 tablespoon butter, 1 shallot, 5 tablespoons herb cream cheese, 1 tsp. Worcestershire sauce, salt, pepper.

Preparation: Boil potatoes in salt water until done. Cut pork filet in slices and brown in oil. Remove from pan and keep warm. Drain oil from pan, add butter and sauté shallot. Add cream cheese, salt, pepper, and Worcestershire sauce to taste. Add meat slices. Put on plate with potatoes (best eaten with peel).

Sauerkraut with Mashed Potatoes

Ingredients: 2 medium-size potatoes, 1 apple, 1 tangerine, 1 tsp. raisin, 4 oz. (125 g) sauerkraut, 1 tablespoon cream, 3 tablespoons milk, salt, pepper, ground nutmeg.

Preparation: Boil potatoes with peel in a little salt water. Dice apple and tangerines and mix with raisins and sauerkraut. Steam in a little water for 12 minutes. Stir in cream. Heat milk, peel potatoes, mash with milk, then fluff with fork. Add salt, pepper, and nutmeg to taste. Serve with sauerkraut.

Try sauerkraut a little differently: Tangerines and raisins
promise a new, exciting taste.

Dinner

You should have a lot of protein and little carbohydrates for dinner. You should eat nothing else after dinner. Before dinner, you will again drink a small glass of water with apple vinegar (without honey). Until you go to bed, you can have herbal tea, carbonated water, vegetable or tomato juice. You can have as much as you want (but no sugar; only sugar substitute in tea is allowed).

Baked Mozzarella

Ingredients: 1 pack of mozzarella, 1 egg, salt, pepper, 2 tablespoons bread crumbs, 2 tsp. butter, 1 slice whole grain bread, 1 small tomato, 1 tsp. lemon juice.
Preparation: Dry mozzarella with a paper towel. Beat egg; add salt and pepper; dip mozzarella in egg mixture, then in bread crumbs. Heat butter in pan; fry mozzarella on both sides until it starts melting. Put on slice of whole grain bread and add sliced tomato. Dribble lemon juice on top.

Shrimp with Scrambled Egg

Ingredients: 1 3/4 oz. (50 g) shrimp, 1 egg, 1 tablespoon cream, 1 tsp. butter, 3 slices of whole grain toast, salt, pepper, paprika, nutmeg, 1 tsp. chopped parsley.
Preparation: Wash shrimp and boil; drain in colander and peel when cooled. Beat egg together with cream and spices. Heat butter in pan, stir in egg mixture and fry. Spread this on toast and top with shrimp. Decorate with chopped parsley.

Potatoes especially contain high-quality carbohydrates. The best is to have them for lunch. At night you should choose dishes high in protein.

Chicory Salad With Egg

Ingredients: 1 avocado, 1 tsp. lemon juice, 2 chicories, 3 tablespoons cream, 1 tablespoon honey, a few drops apple vinegar, salt, 2 slices pumpernickel, 1 tsp. butter.
Preparation: Peel avocado, slice and add some lemon juice. Cut chicory leaves in strips and put on plate with avocado slices. Make a fine sauce by stirring cream, honey, apple vinegar, and salt together; pour over salad. Spread butter on pumpernickel and serve with salad.

Tofu Sausage with Salad

Ingredients: 1 egg, 3 1/2 oz. (100 g) mixed salad of the season, 2 tablespoons vegetable oil, a little apple vinegar, 2 slices of whole grain bread, 1 tsp. butter, 2 tofu sausages, 1 tsp. light mayonnaise.
Preparation: Boil egg until hard and slice. Wash salad and marinate with oil and vinegar, putting sliced egg on top. Spread butter on whole grain bread, top with sliced tofu sausage, and dress with light mayonnaise.

Fruit Cheese with Whole Grain Toast

Ingredients: 1 pear, 1 tangerine, 1 kiwi, 1 banana, 1 tablespoon honey, 7 oz. (200 g) cottage cheese, 3 slices whole grain toast, 1 tsp. raisins.
Preparation: Dice pear, tangerine, kiwi, and banana. Mix with cottage cheese and honey. Spread on toast and top with raisins.

A simple scrambled egg can be prepared in a new way with shrimp. Add pepper, paprika, and parsley to taste, but salt sparingly.

Get Slim in the Long Run

Don't neglect your body during the three-day apple vinegar diet. Every form of activity further enhances the lipolysis (fat-freeing process) from your fat areas. Exercise is, therefore, an ideal way to support the three-day apple vinegar diet. But exercise is not just exercise.

In the following, you will find a few tips about how to get your body fit the right and healthy way. Don't look at these as exercises, but rather as fun.

- *Athletic records are not important. The goal rather, is to reach your personal limit four times a day, and to sweat a little.*

- *Ideal example: Find a set of stairs; for the unfit, 10 steps are enough. Run up and down those stairs until you are out of breath and you start to perspire. This is all it takes.*

- *If you like to ride a bike, then ride it to work, school, or appointments. Or go for a little ride on the weekend. Again: It is not the length or difficulty of the trip, but the fact that you reached your personal limit.*

- *Rope-jumping, knee-bends, push-ups, or sit-ups are alternatives.*

- *For sit-ups, lie on your back and lift your legs. Put your hands under your head and lift your back up, then release it back down. Keep your back straight! Repeat this exercise as often as you can.*

- *Please don't overdo it. The fat from the stomach and hip area is not directly burned with these exercises. But what is important: The active stress on the muscles increases the rate of metabolism.*

- *The stress hormones will suck triglycerides from the fat areas even an hour after you've exercised.*

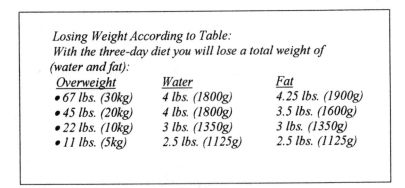

Losing Weight According to Table:
With the three-day diet you will lose a total weight of (water and fat):

Overweight	Water	Fat
• 67 lbs. (30kg)	4 lbs. (1800g)	4.25 lbs. (1900g)
• 45 lbs. (20kg)	4 lbs. (1800g)	3.5 lbs. (1600g)
• 22 lbs. (10kg)	3 lbs. (1350g)	3 lbs. (1350g)
• 11 lbs. (5kg)	2.5 lbs. (1125g)	2.5 lbs. (1125g)

To lose weight, you don't have to set any records. What is more important is that you sweat, and that you reach your personal limit, but the exercise should be fun, not torture.

Seven-Day Apple Vinegar Diet

With this weight loss plan, the diet becomes an offensive against excess pounds that have settled around the belly button, and begins to finally release the fat cells in the area above the knees. Many people have 60 percent of their body weight in this area.

A Double Strategy That Makes You Slim

The Seven-Day apple vinegar diet is based on a slimness recipe of Mother Nature, a double strategy of dehydrating potassium and fat-reducing protein. Important rule: Salt remains reduced, and it only functions as a carrier for iodine, a necessary supplier of sodium. The maximum is 1 teaspoon of iodized salt per day. Beverages include: vegetables and tart fruit drinks, carbonated water, diet lemonade, coffee, green or black tea without sugar and cream (sugar substitute allowed), herbal tea, milk, not more than 16 oz. (1/2 liter) of beer, or 8 oz. (1/4 liter) of dry wine per day.

What You Can Eat

For breakfast you can have whole grain bread, pumpernickel, or whole grain toast. Stay away from mixed and white bread. Never eat whole grain rolls because they contain a fairly high amount of mixed or white flour. Approximately ten minutes before breakfast, you should have a small glass of water, or carbonated water, with a tablespoon of apple vinegar. A very important difference is the substantially higher amount of protein you are allowed in your breakfast compared to the ones you are used to.

Breakfast Offerings

You can create your own breakfast using your imagination. Choose from the following selection those foods that you feel hungry for the most:

- 1 slice of whole grain bread or pumpernickel, 4 slices of whole grain toast
- 2 oz. (60 g) of meat, fish, poultry, or tofu
- All natural vegetables such as tomatoes, cucumbers, radishes, white radishes, paprika, or melon
- All tart fruits such as kiwi, grapefruit, oranges, grapes, berries, apples, plums, or even 1 banana, 1 fresh fig, or olives
- 1 egg (in all possible varieties, also in a little butter, e.g., scrambled or fried)
- Low-fat cheese, curd cheese, yogurt (yogurt is best)

Toast With Prosciutto

Ingredients: 3 slices whole grain toast, 1 tsp. butter, 1 tsp. catsup, 2 oz. (60 g) lean raw or cooked prosciutto, 5 radishes, salt, pepper.
Preparation: Spread butter and catsup on slices of bread. Put prosciutto on each of the bread slices. Wash radishes, slice and place on top of prosciutto. Add pepper and very little salt.

A good start to the day is best accomplished with a good breakfast. Vary the ingredients mentioned above to go with your favorite breakfast.

Tofu With Egg

Ingredients: 1 egg, 1 slice whole grain bread, 1 tsp. butter, 1 tsp. light mayonnaise, 2 tofu sausages, 1 tablespoon chopped parsley.
Preparation: Boil egg until hard and slice. Spread butter and light mayonnaise on bread. Slice tofu sausage and put on bread together with sliced egg. Top sandwich with parsley.

Curd Cheese With Cream and Grapes

Ingredients: 1 cup low-fat curd cheese, 1 tsp. lemon juice, 1 tsp. cream, 3 1/2 oz. (100 g) red or green grapes, 1 tsp. sunflower seeds, 3 slices toast.
Preparation: Mix low-fat curd cheese with lemon juice and cream. Wash grapes and chop. Mix grapes and sunflower seeds with cheese mixture. Serve with toast.

Kiwi With Sour Milk

Ingredients: 1 kiwi, 1 tsp. raisins, 1 tsp. honey, 3 tablespoons oatmeal, 1 cup sour milk, 1 slice pumpernickel.
Preparation: Chop kiwi and add to sour milk, together with raisins, honey, and oatmeal. Serve with pumpernickel.

A good start to the day is best accomplished with a good breakfast. Vary the ingredients mentioned above to go with your favorite breakfast.

Roast Beef and Roasted Beef

Ingredients: 1 slice of whole grain bread, 1 tsp. light mayonnaise, 1 vinegar pickle, 1 thin slice roast beef (1 oz. [30 g]), 1 thin slice roasted beef (different kinds), parsley or dill.

Preparation: Cut whole grain bread into two halves, spread with light mayonnaise. Slice vinegar pickle thinly and place in the middle of each slice of bread. Roll beef slices as tightly as possible and put on sandwich. If you wish, you may decorate it with parsley or dill.

Snacks

For snacks, only carbohydrates should be eaten, which the metabolism needs as well. But only complex carbohydrates are useful - those that are contained in grain. Therefore, you should - no later than 11 am - eat some cereal with grain, containing oats, barley, rye, wheat, buckwheat, or millet. It is ideal to grind your grain yourself with a grinder and let the ground grain soak overnight. If it is presoaked, the intestines can digest it better. Mix the cereal the next morning with fruit, yogurt, or sour milk.

Who likes to get up early? A tasty and lovingly prepared breakfast, with creamy curd cheese and fruit, makes getting up easier. Even morning grouches are more alert!

Lunch

It is important that lunch contain a combination of vegetables and small portions of fish, meat, or poultry (each no more than 1 3/4 oz. [50 grams]). Vegetarians can use soy or tofu products (3 1/2 oz. [100 grams]). Steam the vegetables only briefly in water. The body is provided with the necessary carbohydrates by eating potatoes with peel, natural rice, or whole grain noodles. Appetizers and desserts should be avoided at all cost.

You can drink one cup (1/4 liter) of water or carbonated water enriched with a tablespoon of apple vinegar. Drink one-half of the beverage before lunch, the other half with lunch.

Veal a la Romana

Ingredients: 3 1/2 oz. (100 g) whole grain noodles, 1 3/4 oz. (50 g) lean veal (very thin slices), 3/4 oz. (20 g) lean cooked ham, 2 sage leaves, 1 tablespoon vegetable oil, salt, pepper, catsup. Preparation: Boil noodles in salt water ala dente. Salt and pepper veal. Cut ham in strips and put together with sage leaves on top of veal. Fry in hot oil on both sides. Put on plate together with whole grain noodles; add a little catsup.

You should buy biograins from your whole food store and grind them yourself right before you use them. Grains from traditional farms have to be cleansed thoroughly before use, but here you could lose important ingredients that are contained in the hull.

Prawn in Garlic With Rice

Ingredients: 4 tablespoons natural rice, 1 bundle parsley, 2 garlic cloves, 1 3/4 oz. (50 g) prawn tails, 1 tablespoon butter, salt, pepper, 1 tsp. lemon juice.
Preparation: Boil rice ala dente. Chop parsley. Press garlic cloves and mix with prawn tails; let sit for 10 minutes. Heat butter and fry prawn tails with garlic for 4 minutes. Add salt and pepper and dribble lemon juice over top. Serve together with natural rice.

Potatoes with Liver

Ingredients: 3 potatoes, 1 small slice of veal liver, 1 tablespoon milk, 1 onion, 1 tablespoon parsley, 1 tablespoon savory, 1 tablespoon butter, salt.
Preparation: Boil potatoes. Wash liver and let soak in milk. Chop onion, parsley, and savory. Dry liver and dip into herb mixture. Heat butter and fry liver briefly on both sides. Salt slightly and serve with potatoes.

Whole Grain Spaghetti with Tomato Sauce

Ingredients: 8 3/4 oz. (250 g) whole grain spaghetti, 26 oz. (750 g) tomatoes, 1 oz. (30 g) butter, salt, pepper, 1 bunch basil, 1 3/4 oz (50 g) ground Parmesan cheese.
Preparation: Boil spaghetti in salt water ala dente. Peel and dice tomatoes. Heat some butter in a pot, add tomatoes, and simmer while stirring. Add salt, pepper, and basil to taste. Mix spaghetti with the remaining butter and tomato sauce. Cover with Parmesan cheese.

Everybody loves spaghetti. You don't have to give that up for your diet, but only whole grain spaghetti is allowed.

Spinach with Potatoes and Eggs

Ingredients: 4 potatoes, 3 eggs, 10 1/2 oz. (300 g) leaf spinach, 1 garlic clove, 1 tsp. butter, salt, pepper, nutmeg.
Preparation: Boil potatoes until done. Boil eggs until they reach a wax-like consistency. Wash spinach and boil in pot until it gets mushy; then chop spinach. Press garlic clove and sauté in pot with butter. Add spinach, some salt, pepper, and nutmeg. Peel potatoes and serve with eggs and spinach.

Afternoon

When you lose fat, this usually leads to loud protests from your fat depots. These depots are constantly being provided with more triglycerides. As a consequence, you will usually be craving food, which will be very hard to resist.

A network of hormonal signalizing substances is responsible for these cravings for snacks. The signalizing substances connect intestines, liver, brain, and fat cells. The cravings mostly occur during the afternoon at a time when we are used to eating a slice of tort or cake with whipped cream. When these attacks occur during your seven-day apple vinegar diet, you should fight them with the following snacks:

Coffee and cake should be exceptions, reserved for holidays, and not an everyday ritual. Still, your hunger can be satisfied with little snacks, such as yogurt, fruit or nuts.

- yogurt or low-fat curd cheese
- fruit
- 1 tablespoon nuts, seeds, soy snacks, or trail food
- toast

Dinner

Tasty salad platters and huge bowls of raw vegetables should dominate the last main meal of the day. Make dinner a happy and beautiful event: Set the table lovingly, use the "good" dishes, and give yourself some peace and quiet - you deserve it.

Make the salad dressing from apple vinegar and high-quality vegetable oil with unsaturated fatty acids, e.g., olive oil.

You may have anything, from tuna to smoked tongue, from hard-boiled eggs to smoked tofu, which will increase your appetite for green, yellow, and red vegetables. Reward yourself on a well-disciplined diet day with a few small slices of French bread.

Colorful Raw Vegetable Plate

Ingredients: 1 carrot, 1 small fennel root, 5 olives, 1 portion of salad, 1 tomato, 1 tablespoon vegetable oil, 1 tsp. lemon juice, 1 tsp. apple vinegar, 1 tablespoon chopped parsley, salt, 2 oz. (60 g) salmon, 5 slices French bread.
Preparation: Wash, scrub and chop salad. Peel and dice tomato. Put

Two warm meals a day are an exaggeration: Have a big salad plate or a raw vegetable plate for dinner. If you set the table lovingly, it will taste twice as good.

all on a big plate. Mix a dressing with oil, lemon juice, apple vinegar, and parsley, as well as some salt, and pour over salad. Cut salmon in strips. Serve together with French bread.

Salad with Crab and Eggs

Ingredients: 1 3/4 oz. (50 g) crab, 1 egg, 3 1/2 oz. (100 g) greens, 1 tablespoon apple vinegar, 2 tablespoons sunflower oil, salt, pepper, 1 tablespoon sunflower seeds, 1 slice pumpernickel.
Preparation: Wash crab, boil, drain and dry with paper towel. Boil egg until hard and slice. Wash salad and decorate with egg slices and crab. Make a salad dressing with apple vinegar, oil, a little salt and pepper. Pour over salad, then cover with sunflower seeds. Serve with pumpernickel.

Avocado with Chicory and Prosciutto

Ingredients: 1 chicory, 1 avocado, 1 tsp. lemon juice, 2 table-spoons apple vinegar, salt, pepper, 1 tablespoon vegetable oil, 1 1/2 oz. (40 g) prosciutto, 3 slices whole grain toast, 1 tsp. butter.
Preparation: Chop chicory and avocado; add a little lemon juice to avocado and mix with the chicory. Prepare dressing with apple vinegar, salt, pepper and vegetable oil; pour over chicory-avocado salad. Let it sit for awhile. Roll prosciutto and cut into slices. Spread butter on bread and serve all together.

Egg Salad

Ingredients: 1 salad cucumber, 1 portion of endive salad, 1 tomato, 2 eggs, 4 tablespoons yogurt, 1 tablespoon sour cream, 1 tsp. lemon juice, 1 tablespoon apple vinegar, 1 tsp. honey, salt, 1 slice pumpernickel.

Preparation: Wash cucumber thoroughly, half, take seeds out, and cut into strips. Wash endive, scrub and chop. Peel tomatoes and dice. Boil eggs until hard and slice. Mix all in big glass bowl. Make a salad dressing from the remaining ingredients, add spices to taste, and pour over salad. Serve salad with pumpernickel.

Delicious Tofu

Ingredients: 4 1/3 oz. (125 g) smoked tofu, 1 slice roast or corned beef, 1 oz. (30 g) sheep cheese, 1 tomato, 5 black olives, 1 tablespoon apple vinegar, 1 tablespoon vegetable oil, 1 tsp. lemon juice, salt, pepper, 1 big salad leaf, 3 slices whole grain toast.

Preparation: Dice tofu, cold beef, sheep cheese, and tomato and mix with olives. Make a dressing with apple vinegar, oil, lemon juice, some salt and pepper, and pour over mixture. Let sit for a while. Then mix everything, and put on top of salad leaf. Serve together with whole grain toast.

Tofu is not just a meat substitute for vegetarians. Try a mixed salad platter with this healthy soy product yourself

Exercise and Meditation

Train Yourself Fit and Slim

You can support the seven-day apple vinegar diet with a small fitness program:

- Sweat twice daily with a small three-minute program. Do some rowing while on your back with your legs angled, or do sit-ups, push-ups, knee-bends, stretching exercises, light weight lifting, rope-jumping, etc. Your breaks should never be longer than 10 seconds. Listen to your favorite song and, if possible, exercise until the song ends.
- Other fitness programs will work well, i.e., jazz dancing, aerobics, climbing stairs, stairmaster, pull-ups, etc.
- It is very good to walk 20 minutes daily. Jogging, or riding a bike outside in the sun, is also good, or walk quickly on a slightly rising terrain until your muscles start hurting a little.
- Recommendation: Do these exercises even when it's cold or raining, even though you may get wet. Go home, take a shower, and then rub yourself dry. This activates the slimness genes.

Half an hour of daily relaxation is beneficial to your nerves, and it also increases the activity of your stomach and intestines. Slim-making biological substances enter the blood from the intestinal tract and stomach during these periods of rest.

Medetative Quiet

Immediately after a main meal (after lunch, or better, after dinner) drink a small glass of water to which you have added a tablespoon of apple vinegar. Then go by yourself for a walk in the great outdoors, or a park, and meditate for half an hour.

- Listen to the birds sing
- Watch the clouds glide across the sky
- Watch the tips of the trees sway in the wind
- Listen to the murmur of a river
- Look at a pasture
- Listen to the music of the crickets.

This is How Your Body Reacts

While meditating, you initiate numerous healthy reactions in your body:

- The excessive stimulation of the sympathetic nerve on the vegetative nerve system is decreased. The heart rate is reduced. The blood vessels widen. Stomach and intestinal activity is stimulated. The production of the stress hormone adrenaline in the suprarenal gland is reduced.
- The production of insulin in the pancreas is increased. Under the influence of the hormone insulin, great amounts of substances generating energy (protein, glucose) are sent into muscle tissue and connective tissue.
- Now the metabolism provides all 70 trillion body cells with valuable substances.
- The nerve system slows down and becomes quieter.

- It is only after 30 minutes of meditation that the stream of biological substances from the intestines into the blood and to the fat cells are at their full capacity. Therefore you should not interrupt your meditation any earlier. During this phase, the so-called parasympathicus affects the nerve system. You feel relaxed, refreshed, calm, and full of energy.

Four-Week Apple Vinegar Diet

Lipolysis - Setting Fat Free

Now the great war against those fat areas begins, because there is no longer the opportunity for those lost pounds to return. The formula for this long-term program is: apple vinegar plus lipolytical substances. Lipolytical stands for setting fat free. The body orders certain molecules or biological substances to control the mechanism of lipogenesis and lipolysis in the fat depots.

Food That Makes You Slim

The menu for the four-week apple vinegar diet is built almost exclusively on foods that are rich in lipolytic substances. A great part of these consist of those foods that Mother Nature gave animals to stay fit and trim.

Foods that disturb the natural slimming process:

- *Sugar, sweets, sweet beverages, and even sweet fruit juices*
- *Sausage, fatty meats*
- *Fat sauces, dressings, dip, mayonnaise*
- *Cakes, torts, sweet baked products*
- *French fries, polished rice*
- *Finger foods, pretzels, and salted nuts*
- *Pastries made from lightly-colored flour, such as white bread*
- *Creamy foods, puddings, sweet desserts, ice cream*

Your shopping list during this diet should include the following:

- Oysters, avocados, bananas, berries (blue and red), borage oil, buckwheat, eggs, figs, fish, poultry, vegetables (especially green, red, and yellow), green leafy vegetables, heart, peas and beans, cold water fish, potato and vegetable peels, seeds, crab, liver, lean meat, low-fat cheese, seafood, iodized salt, milk, natural rice, kidneys, nuts, fruits, bell peppers, mushrooms, roots, soy products, whole grain products, tofu products.
- The high quality protein in these foods dissolves under the influence of apple vinegar. This is also true for sauces, dressings, dip, marinades, mayonnaise, etc., if vinegar was used to make it sour.

Helpers for Your Diet: Sun and Iodine

Sun, or daylight, is an important component of this diet. The photons (light particles) need only eight minutes for their long journey from the sun to the earth. The photons hurry through the universe with light speed, and meet the human skin. Here they initiate an important process in the body, for inside the skin cells, vitamin D is formed with the help of cholesterol.

If you want to say goodbye to excess weight, here is an easy and effective solution; the four-week apple vinegar diet mainly employs, besides apple vinegar, fat-freeing (lipolytic) foods.

Get Slim With Sunlight

These "messengers of the sun" enrich, via the blood, every body cell with thousands of trillions of molecules of vitamin D - and that after only two minutes of walking in the sun, especially around noon. Without any sunlight, no vitamin D can be produced inside the human body. Inside the approximately 70 trillion cells, vitamin D enters into the cell nucleus and stimulates vitalizing and slimming genes. In other words, the sun is a very important slim-maker of Mother Nature. But be careful: Too many of the golden rays can reduce the production of vitamin D.

Slim with Iodine

The thyroid gland needs the mineral iodine (e.g. in iodized salt) to produce the hormone thyroxin, another important "slimmaker". Thyroxin is another of the very few molecules that has the key to the gene of the cell nucleus, where it initiates vitalizing and slimming processes. An ample amount of iodine translates into many hormones being produced by the thyroid gland, generating a constant, higher rate of metabolism. These hormones make you feel less tired, keep you fit, and remove excess fat from the problem areas – the stomach and hips.

A sun bath, taken within certain perimeters, is very healthy: Together with cholesterol, the sun rays create vitamin D in the human body, which in turn is a very important stimulant of the slimness genes.

Get Slim With Cold

Before going out for a walk, or any other physical activity, don't dress too warmly. An ideal scenario would be: dress lightly when you leave the house, and then walk or run to defeat the cold. The rule is: You don't lose weight by sweating, but by being chilled!

- Don't avoid bad weather, but seek it out, because the cold stimulates fat-burning stress hormones.
- Don't cover up too warmly in bed, but just enough so you will neither sweat nor freeze.
- Cool or cold beverages (e.g., milk and herbal tea) support the weight loss process more than warm, or hot beverages.

What You Can Eat

- Start your breakfast with a small glass of unsweetened water, adding 1 tsp. apple vinegar.
- Since this diet includes mostly food containing protein after 6 p.m., the stomach will growl in the morning - the brain and nerves demand glucose. This is contained in whole grain bread, pumpernickel, and toast in great quantities.
- Have 2 oz. (60 g) of ham, corned beef, roast beef, smoked tongue, chicken (never with skin), smoked fish filets, tuna, salmon, curd cheese, and low-fat cheese, as well as

People prone to colds should dress warmly in cold weather, but to lose weight, a little chill is ideal. Just walk to get warm.

3.5 oz. (100 grams) smoked tofu, tofu sausage or other tofu products (from your whole food store) with your bread.
- Treat yourself to an egg every second day.
- To burn stomach fat, minerals, high-quality fatty acids and vitamins are necessary. These important substances are contained in bananas, avocados, or in vegetables such as radishes, white radishes, cucumbers, tomatoes, or melons.

Breakfast

Cream Cheese with Fruit

Ingredients: 3.5 oz. (100 g) strawberries, 1 tsp. lemon juice, 1 cup cottage cheese, 1 tablespoon cream, 1 tablespoon sunflower seeds, 1 slice pumpernickel.
Preparation: Wash strawberries and dice. Add lemon juice and let sit for a few minutes. Mix cottage cheese with cream and strawberries. Sprinkle sunflower seeds on top. Eat with pumpernickel.

Cold Beef Breakfast

Ingredients: 1 slice whole grain bread, 1 tsp. butter, 2 oz. (60 g) cold beef, 1 tsp. light mayonnaise, 1 tomato.
Preparation: Spread butter on bread. Put cold beef on top and decorate with light mayonnaise. Wash tomato, slice and put on bread.

A tasty breakfast for strawberry fans: cottage cheese with fresh strawberries, cream, and lemon juice. Breakfast also tastes good with other fruits of the season.

Roast Beef With Egg

Ingredients: 1 slice of roast beef, 1 egg, 3 slices toast, 1 tsp. butter, 1 small vinegar pickle, 1 tablespoon light mayonnaise, fresh herbs (e.g., chives, parsley).
Preparation: Cut roast beef in strips. Boil egg until hard and slice. Spread butter on bread and add egg and roast beef strips. Dice vinegar pickle and distribute on sandwich. Add light mayonnaise and fresh herbs to taste.

Avocado With Whole Grain Bread

Ingredients: 1 1/2 avocados, 1 tsp. lemon juice, salt, pepper, 1 slice whole wheat bread.
Preparation: Cut avocado in half, separate and take pit out. Take one half and remove fruit flesh with a spoon. Mash flesh with fork. Dribble lemon juice over the mashed avocado; add salt, pepper and let sit for a short time. Spread avocado mash on bread; add salt and pepper to taste.

Shepherd's Breakfast

Ingredients: 1 tomato, 1 egg, 5 slices of cucumber/pickle, 1 3/4 oz. (50 g) sheep cheese, 5 olives, pepper, paprika, 1 slice whole grain bread.
Preparation: Wash and slice tomato. Boil egg until hard and slice. Put on bread together with cucumber/pickle slices, sheep cheese, olives and spices.

*Avocados contain more potassium than any other food. That is
the reason why they create beauty from the inside.*

Snacks

In the Morning

Cereal is recommended as a healthy and slimming snack for the morning:

- For that, mix *1/2* cup (225 g) of self-ground grain (choose from oats, barley, wheat, buckwheat, or millet) with cream, chopped fruit, nuts, seeds.
- You can also add some raisins, honey, or molasses syrup (from your whole food store), but you should not sweeten your cereal too much.

In the Afternoon

Now we recommend acetic protein snacks. There are many combinations to choose from:

- Mushrooms marinated in vinegar
- Marinated appetizers from the delicatessen store
- 1 slice cold beef, roast beef, lean ham, smoked tongue, or turkey with mixed pickles
- Tofu sausage with mustard
- Egg salad, or a small bowl of sliced mushrooms in apple vinegar dressing

You should grind cereal only shortly before you use it. Due to air and light, valuable nutrients are lost when stored for a longer time period. Cereal that has been soaked overnight can be digested much easier.

- Toast with butter
- Tomato slices and light mayonnaise
- Sheep cheese marinated in oil and vinegar
- Vinegar pickle with marinated herring, or salt herring

Lunch

Have a glass of water with apple vinegar before lunch, and then another one right after lunch. Don't drink anything else for lunch. The acid pH level of the stomach liquids should not be diluted with too many other liquids. Here are the ideal (lipolytic) foods:

- fish
- green leafy vegetables
- mushrooms
- fruit
- low-fat cheese

Trout with Potatoes

Ingredients: 4 potatoes, 1 small trout, salt, 1 tablespoon lemon juice, 1 bundle parsley, 1 tablespoon white wine, 1 tablespoon sour cream.
Preparation: Boil potatoes in jacket until done. Wash trout, salt inside and out, and dribble lemon juice on top. Stuff with parsley and lay out on a piece of aluminum foil. Pour white wine over it, then wrap trout in foil. Bake in the oven at 400^0 F (200^0 C) for approximately 40 minutes. Pour juice from the aluminum foil over potatoes. Pour sour cream over potatoes and enjoy.

Natural Rice with Broccoli

Ingredients: 4 tablespoons natural rice, 10 1/2 oz. (300 g) broccoli, pepper, salt, 1 tablespoon white wine, 2 tablespoons butter, 1 tablespoon chopped almonds, 1 tablespoon almond slivers.

Preparation: Boil rice a la dente. Wash broccoli, separate "flowers", and cut stems into strips. Steam all in salt water. Add pepper and a little salt. Add wine, and let steam with closed lid for 20 minutes. Melt butter, add almonds and roast. Pour over broccoli and serve together with natural rice. Decorate with almond slivers.

Leek With Salad

Ingredients: 1 liter vegetable broth, 1 3/4 oz. (50 g) butter, 2 3/4 oz. (80 g) ground "green seed", 2 eggs, 2 tsp. fresh ground pepper, salt, nutmeg, 1 3/4 oz. (50 g) leek, 1/2 cup cream, 1 1/2 oz. (40 g) Parmesan.

Preparation: Heat vegetable broth. Soften butter, then add "green seed" and eggs, stir with fork, and add spice mixture to taste. Let sit for 1/2 hour. Make dumplings from dough and put in simmering vegetable broth. Let sit for 15 minutes after they surface. Let them dry thoroughly before putting them into a buttered casserole dish. Clean leek, cut into rings, mix with cream and pour over dumplings. Put Parmesan on top. Bake in oven at 400^0 F (200^0 C) for approximately 15 minutes.

*Prepare green vegetables differently: broccoli steamed in
white wine, and covered with roasted almond slivers,
makes a tasty side dish with natural rice.*

Tasty Fish Stew

Ingredients: 4 tablespoons natural rice, 2 oz. (60 g) fish, 1 tablespoon lemon juice, 1/2 green bell pepper, 1 tomato, 1 tsp. butter, 1/2 cup vegetable broth, 1 tsp. tomato paste, thyme, salt, pepper, 1 tablespoon sour cream.
Preparation: Boil rice in salt water. Cut fish filet into small pieces and add drops of lemon juice. Let sit for a little while. Cut bell pepper into strips. Heat butter and brown fish pieces, add salt, and steam with vegetables. Add tomato paste to vegetable broth, stir well and add to fish-vegetable mixture. Add sour cream and serve with rice.

Leaf Spinach With Veal Liver

Ingredients: 9 oz. (250 g) leaf spinach, nutmeg, salt, pepper, 1 tablespoon Parmesan, 1 onion, 1 tsp. butter, 2 oz. (60 g) veal liver, 4 slices French bread.
Preparation: Wash and steam spinach until soft. Let drain and chop. Add nutmeg, salt, pepper, and sprinkle with cheese. Cut onion into rings and sauté in butter until golden brown. Brown veal liver on both sides, add salt and pepper, and serve with spinach and onion rings. Eat with French bread.

The healthy "green seed" vegetable is slowly coming back into fashion. Try some "green seed" dumplings with melted cheese over leek. Maybe you will like it too.

Dinner

For dinner, you will have less carbohydrates, but more protein. The rule is: Carbohydrates make fat, protein slims. Therefore, you can't have much bread - a few slices of French bread or 2 slices whole grain toast.

During the meal, you can have a glass of water or carbonated water with half a tablespoon apple vinegar.
Your meal plan for dinner also includes:

- Fish, crab
- Lean meat, poultry (without skin)
- Tofu products
- Low-fat cheese
- Raw vegetables
- Salad
- Vegetables that have been steamed, but only briefly

Bell Pepper Salad with Tofu Sausage

Ingredients: 1 each red and green bell pepper, 1 onion, 1 small vinegar pickle, 2 tofu sausages, 1 tsp. mustard, 1 tablespoon apple vinegar, 1 tablespoon vegetable oil, 1 tsp. lemon juice, salt, pepper, 2 slices toast.
Preparation: Cut bell peppers into four parts, wash, remove white separations and seeds, and cut into thin slices. Peel onion and cut into rings. Chop vinegar pickle finely. Slice tofu sausages finely. Put everything in a bowl and mix well. Mix mustard, apple vinegar, vegetable oil, lemon juice, salt, and pepper to make dressing; pour over salad. Serve together with toast.

Salad With Smoked Tongue

Ingredients: 2 oz. (60 g) smoked tongue, 2.5 oz. (70 g) salad, 2 tablespoons vegetable oil, 1 tablespoon apple vinegar, salt, pepper, 1 tablespoon sunflower seeds, fresh herbs, 2 slices whole grain toast, 1 tsp. butter.

Preparation: Chop smoked tongue into small pieces. Clean salad leaves, let dry, and mix with chopped tongue. Make dressing from vegetable oil, apple vinegar, salt and pepper; pour over salad. Roast sunflower seeds and sprinkle on top. Decorate salad with fresh herbs to taste. Toast bread, spread with butter, and serve together with salad.

Raw Fennel with Shrimp

Ingredients: 2 oz. (60 g) shrimp, 1 tsp. lemon juice, 1 fennel root, 3 tablespoons cream, 1 tsp. tomato paste, pepper, 2 slices toast.

Preparation: Wash shrimp with lots of water, then let dry. Add lemon juice and let this sit for a few minutes. Wash and clean fennel root and cut into small strips. Mix fennel and shrimp in a bowl. Slightly whip cream and make dressing with lemon juice, tomato paste, and pepper. Add spices to taste and pour dressing over shrimp-fennel salad. Serve salad with toast.

Salads low in carbohydrates and high in protein are excellent for dinner. Depending on what you like, you can choose from recipes with or without meat.

Raw Vegetable Platter With Tuna

Ingredients: 2 oz. (60 g) tuna (from a can), 9 oz. (250 g) celery, 7 oz. (200 g) red beets, 1 orange, 1 tablespoon apple vinegar, 2 tablespoons vegetable oil, salt, pepper, 1 tablespoon sunflower seeds, 2 slices whole grain toast, 1 tsp. butter.

Preparation: Let tuna dry and cut into small pieces. Wash and scrub celery and red beets, peel and chop orange, and mix oranges, celery and red beets with tuna. Make dressing from apple vinegar, vegetable oil, salt, pepper, and celery; add spices to taste and pour over raw vegetables. Roast sunflower seeds slightly and sprinkle over salad. Toast bread, spread with butter, and serve together with salad.

Chicken Salad Hong Kong

Ingredients: 2 small tomatoes, 2 oz. (60 g) boiled chicken breast (skinless), 5 oz. (150 g) peach slices, 2 tablespoons apple vinegar, 2 tablespoons vegetable oil, pepper, 1 tsp. curry, 1 tsp. Worcestershire sauce, 3 slices toast.

Preparation: Peal and dice tomatoes. Cut chicken breast into small pieces. Dice peach slices and mix with tomatoes and chicken. Make dressing by mixing apple vinegar, vegetable oil, pepper, curry, Worcestershire sauce, and pour over salad. Let sit for a while before serving with toast.

For all fans of oriental chicken salads, try sweet-sour chicken with peaches, curry, and apple vinegar. Whatever salad you prepare, they all go well with a slice of whole grain bread, or toast.

Raw Vegetables With Cheese

Ingredients: 2 carrots, 2 leek onions, salt, pepper, some parsley, 2 slices whole grain toast, 1 tsp. butter, 1 3/4 oz. (50 g) cheese with caraway seed, 1 avocado, 1 tablespoon apple vinegar.

Preparation: Clean carrots and leek onions and quarter. Sprinkle with a little salt, pepper, and some of the parsley. Toast bread and spread with butter. Decorate with remaining parsley. Slice cheese and put on toast. Cut avocado in half and remove pit. Pour apple vinegar on both avocado halves. Arrange all ingredients nicely on platter.

Losing Weight According to Table:
With the four-week diet you will lose a total weight of (water and fat):

Overweight	Water	Fat
• 67 lbs (30kg)	4.5 lbs. (2000g)	9.5 lbs. (4300g)
• 45 lbs. (20kg)	4.5 lbs. (2000g)	6.5 lbs. (2900g)
• 22 lbs. (10kg)	4 lbs. (1800g)	6 lbs. (2700g)
• 11 lbs. (5kg)	3.3 lbs. (1500g)	4.25 lbs. (1900g)

Try a vinaigrette, made from 2 hard boiled eggs, 2 tablespoons vegetable oil, 2 tablespoons apple vinegar, one small chopped onion, pepper, salt, and fresh herbs with your raw vegetables. Mash eggs with a fork and make a dressing by adding the other ingredients - done! The vinaigrette also tastes good with leafy salads, beans, and artichokes.

Apple Vinegar in the Kitchen and Throughout the House

Apple vinegar has many practical advantages besides its healthy healing effects. This holds true in the kitchen, as well as throughout the house.

Kitchen Tricks with Apple Vinegar

- Apple vinegar keeps meats, venison, and poultry fresh longer.
- Apple vinegar tenderizes meat.
- Beans, peas, lentils, and cabbage are easier digested with a little apple vinegar added to them.
- Add apple vinegar to the water in which you wash your vegetables and salads. It disinfects from bacteria, fungi, and other damaging pathogens.
- Apple vinegar is a great ingredient in catsup, dressings, dip, and mayonnaise.
- Apple vinegar enhances the taste of many herbs.
- Apple vinegar adds taste to sauces.
- Apple vinegar removes lime, e.g., in the hot broiler.
- Apple vinegar is great for marinades.
- Apple vinegar enhances the taste of fish broth.
- Apple vinegar keeps cheese fresh longer: Pour some apple vinegar into water and soak a kitchen towel in it. Then wrap the cheese in the towel. Don't use paper or plastic wrap.
- Apple vinegar is a good disinfectant for counters, stoves, tubs, pots, pans, and other kitchen appliances.
- Apple vinegar makes your dishwater free from germs.
- Apple vinegar is very good for conserving vegetables, mushrooms, cucumbers, eggs, meat, etc.

- A little bit of apple vinegar makes egg shells softer, and prevents them from splitting in boiling water.
- Apple vinegar keeps food fresh longer.

Practical Tips Throughout the House

- Apple vinegar as an all-purpose cleaner: It does not just remove dirt and grease, but also odor. It prevents the buildup of mold and it disinfects. One cup in your water bucket is enough.

- Stains are removed easier with apple vinegar. This is especially true for stains from paint, glue, or chewing gum.

- Remove lime stains on flower pots with a rag soaked in apple vinegar.

- In the bathroom, apple vinegar removes even persistent lime stains, e.g., on dies, or in the tub, but also on shower heads and faucets.

- Pour a cup of apple vinegar down your drains every once in a while. This prevents odorous drains, and also keeps them from clogging.

- Remove lime the biological way from appliances such as your iron, or the coffee maker.

  Add a little apple vinegar to your dishwater and your glasses will sparkle again.

You can do more with apple vinegar than just drink it. There are many ways to use it in the kitchen. For example, apple vinegar can be used effectively to remove lime, or to disinfect.

- Wooden cooking tools become totally clean when occasionally rubbed with apple vinegar.

- Natural sponges become soft when washed in warm vinegar water and then rinsed in cold water. In bad cases, leave the sponge in the apple vinegar solution overnight.

- Even brushes made from natural hair can be revived again when soaked in an apple vinegar solution overnight.

- Add a little apple vinegar to your colored laundry to revive the colors.

- Use apple vinegar instead of softener. Just add a little to the water.

- A little apple vinegar in the water of your iron will help to produce better creases.

- Add a little apple vinegar to the water when you boil your Easter eggs; their colors will be much brighter.

Apple vinegar is even good for the water you use to water your plants: Add two tablespoons once weekly to your water for all plants, inside and out. This acts like a natural fertilizer. In your yard, it also helps to keep damaging insects and snails away from your flowers and vegetables.

The Fast Weight Loss – Look at the Animals

Animals in the wild always remain at their best weight. These are the reasons:

- *Avoid Unhealthy Nutrition*
  Animals eat only what their bodies need. Nowhere in the wild can you find hot dogs and french fries, or torts, or lemonade.
- *Cold, and Changes in Temperature*
  Animals are more often exposed to cold. This results in a greater loss of fat molecules. The frequent change of cold phases to long phases of warmth is ideal. That is why not all your rooms should have the same temperature.
- *Room Temperature*
  Metabolism and the process of setting fat free are stimulated when you go from your comfortably warm bathroom, through a cold hallway, to get to your adequately heated office.
- *Not Too Many Clothes*
  Don't wear an extra sweater when you go for a walk, or hike, or even when you go shopping.
- *Vitamin D*
  Sun and daylight produces vitamin D molecules in the skin. Vitamin D enhances the metabolism in the cell nucleuses of the genes. When the metabolism is at a high capacity, the fat around the stomach just "melts" away.
- *Cold Beverages*
  Animals never drink warm beverages. Cold, or at least cool, drinks have a definite influence on the process of losing weight. Substitute the hot coffee or tea with cool beverages, such as apple juice with water, iced tea, or carbonated water.
- *Iodine Supply*
  An adequate supply of iodine is a must for the ample protection of thyroxin in the thyroid gland. Therefore, use only iodized salt, but with care. Without conscious intake of iodine, you will suffer from iodine deficiency. That is why you should have fish at least once weekly in your meal plans.

Animals in the wild never have weight problems because they have a changing supply of food, constant exercise, and daily changes in temperature. This is a good example for your own lifestyle.

The Eleven Best Apple Vinegar Drinks

Healthy and Tasty
Dr. Jarvis Drink

Ingredients: 1 glass fresh water (preferably bottled or purified), 2 tablespoons apple vinegar, 2 tablespoons honey.
Preparation: Mix the water with the apple vinegar and honey.

The Dr. Jarvis Drink was the first drink containing apple vinegar. Because of its simple preparation, this drink holds a cult-like status with apple vinegar. Dr. Forest Clinton Jarvis, a physician from Vermont, made the health-promoting effect of apple vinegar known with this drink.

Water Quality Is Important

Use water from the faucet, but only if you are sure it is fresh, clean, and of high quality. Water is not just water: The fresher the water is, e.g., water from a well, or fresh mountain water, the more active is the combination of water molecules and minerals, or microscopic minerals. Water is not just a combination of classic H_2O molecules (H=hydrogen, O=oxygen), but it is also a complicated structure of hydrogen and oxygen. The water quality is diminished if the water

A true cult-like drink of firm apple vinegar fans is the Dr. Jarvis Drink. Like all other drinks, this one should be prepared with fresh water.

stays too long in pipes or other containers. Ideal would be water from wells or the mountains that you could fill freshly into bottles.

Vinegar-Vegetable Juice

Ingredients: 1 bottle of vegetable juice (24 oz. [0.7 liters]), 2 tablespoons apple vinegar.
Preparation: Stir apple vinegar into vegetable juice and store mixture in a dark bottle.

This drink attacks the adipozytes (fat cells), and therefore increases weight loss. You should drink the contents of the bottle throughout the entire day. It would be ideal if you used vegetable juices you made yourself. It can be said that all kinds of vegetables containing water are better suitable for this drink, e.g., carrots, celery, melons or cucumbers.

Anions and Cations

Apple vinegar activates the numerous nutrients and essences in vegetables especially effectively. This is when vitamins, minerals, and enzymes reach their highest effectiveness.

Apple vinegar contributes to ionize the atoms or molecules contained in the juice, or in other words, to charge them electronically. This creates negatively charged ions, or anions, as are contained in acids and salts, as well as positively loaded cations.

The adding of vinegar to all vegetable juices activates the nutrients and essences of the vegetable. The acid of the vinegar enhances the process of the metabolism that sets fat free.

Anions and cations develop a dynamic lipolytic (setting fat free) effect of metabolism inside the body. This process begins in just half an hour after the consumption of the vegetable juice.

Sour-Cucumber Drink

Ingredients: 1 English cucumber, 1 cup of sorrel, 1 tablespoon dill, 1 large cup of kefir, 1 tablespoon apple vinegar, herb salt, pepper.
Preparation: Peel the English cucumber, dice it, and mix it with other herbs. Add the kefir and the apple vinegar, mix, and add herb salt and pepper to taste.

Jamaica Drink

Ingredients: 10 1/2 oz. (300 g) seasonal fruit, 1/4 liter pineapple juice, 1 tablespoon honey, 1 tablespoon apple vinegar.
Preparation: Wash and dice seasonal fruit and press in juicer. Mix juice with other ingredients

Apple vinegar does not always have to taste like apple vinegar. It also goes well with sweet fruit since it is a product of fruit fermentation.

Pineapple for the Digestion of Protein

Drink this Jamaica drink both before and during meals. The apple vinegar contained in it improves and enhances the absorption of protein. The enzyme bromelain contained in the pineapple juice is especially effective in the upper part of the small intestine.

Bromelain is a proteolytic (protein-splitting) enzyme. Its great advantage is in the fast digestion of all foods that are rich in protein. The vitamin C and the numerous bioflavonoids contained in the fruits and juices further activate the buildup of fat-freeing hormones and enzymes.

The Effective Enzyme Bromelain

Bromelain, the enzyme in pineapple, is a true miracle in its manifold ways to help:

- Bromelain reduces the clotting of blood.
- Bromelain enhances the circulation.
- Bromelain reduces blood pressure.
- Bromelain reduces the clogging of blood vessels that leads to dangerous arteriosclerosis.
- Bromelain reduces the risk of infections.
- Bromelain relaxes muscles.
- Bromelain reduces muscle spasms, such as craps during menstruation.

Combine Your Individual Pineapple Drink

You can vary the recipe of the Jamaica drink to your liking. Pineapple juice and apple vinegar are the basic ingredients: Add citrus juices, but also juices with high percentages of acid, e.g. rhubarb juice, kiwi juice, papaya juice, etc. You can also add any fruit you can imagine. Simply try - you will soon find your personal favorite.

Garden Drink

Ingredients: 2 tomatoes, 3 radishes, 1/2 cucumber, 1 tablespoon apple vinegar, and some chopped dill.

Preparation: Wash tomatoes and remove the green part where the flower was attached. Wash and scrub radishes. Peel cucumber. Put vegetables through juicer, then add apple vinegar to the juice. Decorate with dill, and serve.

This tasty vegetable juice does not just taste good during the summer under a shade tree, but it prevents colds and flu when it gets colder and wetter.

Cleansing the Intestine with Kefir:

The weight loss drink containing kefir (a milk product similar to yogurt) cleans the intestinal environment and takes away a lot of fat; this helps to eliminate the problem of fat accumulating around the stomach or hip area, or around the rear and upper thighs. The facto microbe contained in the kefir, as well as the substances contained in dill and sorrel, all work together with the apple vinegar to detoxicate the small intestines and colon from colonies of fungi and bacteria. This stimulates the peristalsis (intestinal movement). This results in a faster excretion of food remnants, and less fat can be absorbed in the intestines.

Christmas Drink

Ingredients: 1 oz. (25 g) Gluehwein spice (mulled wine spice), 1 liter water, 4 oz. (125 g) dried fruit, 9 oz. (250 g) elderberry juice, 12 oz. (350 g) black current juice, 9 oz. (250 g) apple juice, 1/5 liter raspberry syrup, 3 tablespoons apple vinegar.

Self-made or store-bought kefir is also a highly effective ingredient for weight-loss beverages. Kefir stimulates digestion and reduces fat.

Preparation: Put Gluehwein spice into boiling water, let sit for 15 minutes. Run water through sieve, add dried fruit, and bring to a boil again. Then add all juices, the syrup, and the apple vinegar. Heat again and serve.

When the snow falls, and Christmas nears, punches, grogs, and Gluehwein are among the favorite drinks. The amount of this recipe is enough for the entire family. Since this drink is rich in fruit sugar, only those family members without fat areas should have those Christmas cookies.

Vinegar Tea

Ingredients: 1 liter chamomile or peppermint tea, 2 tablespoons lemon juice, 4 tablespoons honey, 1 tablespoon apple vinegar, and 1 twig lemon balm.

Preparation: Mix tea with lemon juice, honey and apple vinegar. Decorate with twig of lemon balm before serving.

The Coordination of Acids

The acetic acid contained in the apple vinegar, as well as the citric and ascorbic acid of the lemon juice, all complement each other well, and they stimulate the production of gastric acid in the mucous tissue of the stomach. This enhances the utilization of the protein. Certain proteins, such as the stress hormone, are necessary to shrink the fat cells. At the same time, the herbal tea flushes the intestines out, and reduces the absorption of fat through the mucous tissue into the blood.

Vinegar tea is an ideal means to lose weight. It is best to drink after a meal. Vinegar tea is also a great way to cool down on a hot summer day.

Vitalizing Drink

Ingredients: 2 carrots, 1 cucumber, 1 celery root, 1 apple, 1 tablespoon apple vinegar, and iodized salt.
Preparation: Wash carrots, cucumber, celery, and scrub the apple and take out its seeds. Then put all in the juicer. Mix the juice with apple vinegar, and add a little salt to taste. The vitalizing drink especially stimulates the reduction of triglycerides. Apple vinegar and vegetable juice prevent the buildup of too many fat depots. The iodine contained in the salt enhances the production of the hormones produced by the thyroid gland. This, in turn, increases the rate of metabolism in all 70 trillion body cells.

Good Night Drink

Ingredients: 1 liquor glass (1 cup [250 ml]) carbonated water, 1 tsp. apple vinegar.
Preparation: Mix water with apple vinegar.

The good night drink ensures that the pituitary gland increases its production of the growth hormone. To obtain the full benefit of this weight-loss enhancing hormone, you should eat food that is high in protein, e.g., 3/4 oz. (20 g) of chicken, 1 slice of cold cuts, roast beef some fish, or - for vegetarians - some smoked tofu.

The good night drink is an optimal stimulant of the pituitary gland which produces the weight-reducing growth hormones in high quantities after a dinner rich in protein.

The Good Night Drink With Food Rich in Protein

Drink this power mix right before a snack. Two hours later, the amino acids enter the blood and brain at a higher rate. In the pituitary gland, the molecules of the growth hormone are produced. These open up the fat cells at night, and set them free to be burned. The pituitary gland only reaches its full capacity, though, if you have a sufficient amount of protein-rich food before going to bed.

Tomato-Mexico Drink

Ingredients: 3 cups (0.7 liters) tomato juice, 1 tablespoon apple vinegar, pepper, salt, Tabasco, 1 oz. (30 g) creme fraiche, 1 tablespoon herb mix, 1 slice lemon.
Preparation: Mix tomato juice with apple vinegar, then add pepper, salt and Tabasco until it is hot. Add a little creme fraiche to each glass, cover with herbs, and decorate with a slice of lemon.

This Tomato-Mexico drink gets the circulation going. That way, more fat-eating biological substances reach the cells. The consequence: the cell activity is enhanced. The so-called mitochondria are released, especially in the muscle cells.

The triglycerides are destroyed with hot pepper - with a drink that utilizes the wonderful and unique taste of tomatoes:
the Tomato-Mexico drink.

Inside these mitochondria (energy burners) the fat molecules are transformed into energy with the help of different vitamins and minerals. Unwanted fat from the depots is also used in this way.

Summer Fun

Ingredients: 1 cup (1/4 liter) grapefruit juice, 1 cup (1/4 liter) cherry juice, 19 1/2 oz. (500 g) seasonal fruit, 1 quart of carbonated water, 2 tablespoons honey, 3 tablespoons apple vinegar, 1 twig lemon balm.
Preparation: Freeze grapefruit juice and cherry juice separately in freezer (e.g., in cubes). Wash, scrub, and dice all fruit and put in big punch bowl together with fruit juice cubes. Add carbonated water and stir in honey and apple vinegar. Decorate with twig of lemon balm.

This sweet-sour, refreshing drink is great - it simply flushes the fat out of the body. What we need to be aware of is the combination of alcoholic beverages, or sweet drinks, such as lemonade or sodas, together with fat food and pastries containing white flour, causes our weight problems. So drink this tasty, refreshing, and healthy apple vinegar punch without a care.

Wonderful Grapefruit

The great yellow and juicy grapefruits are true health bombs -full of vitamin C. One single ripe grapefruit contains the entire daily supply of vitamin C for an adult. Vitamin C is additionally protected through

On warm summer days, an ice-cold glass of punch tastes best - but without alcohol. Alcohol causes not just a hangover, but also, in combination with fat, weight problems.

bioflavonoids. These bioflavonoids enhance the healing power of vitamin C up to 20 times. It also supplies the body with valuable folic acid. Due to this high concentration of biological substances, the grapefruit has tremendous healing power.

Grapefruit helps with diseases of the blood vessels, varicose veins, and hemorrhoids.

Grapefruit strengthens the immune system and hormone production.

- Grapefruit prevents infections and colds.
- Grapefruit cleans the intestines, and stabilizes the intestinal environment.
- Grapefruit helps with weight-loss diets.

Apple Vinegar Mustard

Apple vinegar enhances weight loss, and it also helps keep you healthy; that is a well-known fact. Stomach, intestines, blood, and cells all profit from the acetic acid, a component of apple vinegar. Apple vinegar is also contained in mustard. That is why mustard is an important means to fight fat cells.

An Unusual Slimmer-Downer

The Romans and Greeks knew about the healing powers of mustard, especially when it came to infections and rheumatic diseases (e.g., by applying mustard poultices). But mustard also helps with constipation and overweight. Mustard is a mild laxative. Apple vinegar, as an additional component of apple vinegar mustard, enhances the effect of this natural slimmer-downer. Mustard and apple vinegar combined act as a miracle weapon against excess weight. The good news is: It is easy to make your own apple vinegar mustard.

Ingredients of Mustard

From a scientific or botanical perspective, there are various kinds of perennial mustard plants: The white, the black, and the brown mustard are the most well-known kinds. The seeds of these plants are also called mustard. Mustard plants can get as tall as 5 feet (1 1/2 meters).

Mustard is a natural remedy against constipation and overweight. Adding apple vinegar enhances its health-promoting effects even further.

Mustard can be bought in tubes or in glass jars. Mustard is derived from mustard seeds; brown and yellow seeds are used. Other ingredients are spices, herbs, salt, sugar, horseradish, or other ingredients, as well as vinegar. The vinegar gives the mustard the necessary acid, and adds to its spicy taste.

Taste Variations

You can produce many specific kinds of mustard by varying the ingredients, especially the spices and herbs:

To create a mustard that is less spicy, you have to reduce the amount of horseradish. This mustard will have a mild aroma.
But if you add a lot of horseradish, then you will have one of the very strong and spicy varieties of mustard.
The acetic acid that is contained in the mustard has an antibacterial effect, as well as an antimycotic (antifungus) one. The same is true for spices like pepper, chili, or horseradish. Therefore, mustard does not need any preservatives to be edible after a long period of time. You can assume that even the industrially produced mustard does not contain any substances to give it its color.

Mustard is produced from mustard seeds, different kinds of spices, vinegar, and horseradish. To achieve varying degrees of spiciness, you vary the amount of horseradish.

Make Your Own Apple Vinegar Mustard

You can buy mustard seeds from a whole food store. You can mix light, or yellow, or brown mustard seeds. You should know that mustard seeds contain 30% or more oils. This oil does not have a distinctive taste, but it does complicate the production of mustard. The typical, spicy taste of mustard is only set free by enzymes when the components without oil come in contact with water. The oil, as well as the vitamin E contained in the oil, will prevent this contact with the water at first. After the seeds are set free, the oil becomes rancid. The sharp, antimicrobial effects of the mustard oil protect the seed only as long as a new mustard plant can grow from it.

Mustard seeds that are separated from the oil can absorb an enormous amount of water. The seeds swell. You can buy mustard powder, as well as mustard seeds, in whole food stores. Mustard powder is much easier to use to produce mustard, because you don't have to grind the seeds before you start this process.

Tips to Produce Mustard

Be aware of the following things when producing mustard:

- Mustard powder is mixed with apple vinegar. Either boil it or stir it to create a mash.
- Only then are the ingredients added that give it its typical taste. Boil again.
- To make sure you don't lose the hot components, pour the final product into glass jars and seal them.
- Store the mustard in a cool and dark place.
- Home-made mustard usually expires after three to six months.

Mustard with Herbs

Ingredients: 9 oz. (250 g) mustard seeds or mustard powder, 1 *3/4* cups (0.4 liters) apple juice, 1 3/4 cups (0.4 liters) apple vinegar, 1 tablespoon herb mix, herb salt.

Preparation: Grind mustard seeds or use mustard powder. Mix the apple juice and apple vinegar, and let sit for one morning or afternoon. Finally, stir in the herb mix and add herb salt to taste.

Paprika Mustard

Ingredients: 9 oz. (250 g) mustard seeds or mustard powder, 1 cup (0.2 liters) apple juice, 0.2 liters apple vinegar, 1 tablespoon paprika, salt, sugar.

Preparation: Grind seeds well, or use mustard powder. Mix with apple juice and apple vinegar. Let sit for two hours. Then add paprika, salt, and some sugar. Heat mass over small flame and bring to a boil while stirring. Stir until a firm mash forms. Pour mustard immediately into glass jars and store in a cool, dark place.

Apple Vinegar Mustard

Ingredients: 9 oz. (250 g) mustard seeds or mustard powder, 1 bottle apple vinegar (25 oz. [0.7 liters]), 1 tablespoon honey, herb salt.

Preparation: Grind seeds, or use mustard powder. Mix with apple vinegar and bring to a boil. Stir constantly. At the same time, add remaining ingredients. Pour into glass jars after it has cooled.

Hot Mustard

Ingredients: 9 oz (250 g) mustard seeds, or mustard powder, 2 tablespoons honey, 1 tsp. pepper, 1 tsp. Tabasco, 1 cup (0.2 liters) apple juice, 1 cup (0.2 liters) apple vinegar, 1 3/4 oz. (50 g) fresh horseradish, herb salt.

Preparation: Grind seeds, or use mustard powder. Mix with apple juice and apple vinegar and let sit for one morning or afternoon. Then add all other ingredients and bring to a boil over medium heat. Stir constantly until it reaches the consistency of mustard. Pour mustard into glass jars and store in a cool, dark place.

To get a really hot mustard, add horseradish, pepper, and Tabasco. If your taste buds are more sensitive, you may be better off with apple vinegar mustard.

More Exercise

If you put all your money on the apple vinegar diet, then you can enhance the lipolysis (fat-freeing) with a targeted exercise concept to optimize the process of losing weight. The acetic acid can fight the fat cells even on its own, but any physical activity gives the process of burning calories an additional kick. A very important factor: exercise programs and apple vinegar enhance each other.

Why Animals Are So Healthy

Only extremely healthy animals survive in the wild. To survive in the cruel environment provided by Mother Nature, each animal - be it rabbit, deer, bird, or fish, has to keep its ideal weight. Animals would not have any excess weight, even if they ate only one kind of food, or only fatty foods. The only exception to this rule would be pregnant mothers, or animals that need to survive in the winter.

Get Fit and Slim

This principle of natural slimness is also included in the human genetic makeup. Because humans are also a product of nature. Our species lived according to the laws of nature before civilization led us down a new path. A natural and healthy program to stay slim is

A lot of exercise and good nutrition are two central building blocks for your slim body. Apple vinegar alone won't get you there.

only interrupted if one's eating habits are contrary to those established by nature. This is often the case in our society where stress and an unhealthy diet prevail.

How to Get Your Metabolism Fit

These are prerequisites for a healthy metabolism:

- Expose yourself to changes in weather and temperature
- Lots of oxygen
- Eat only natural, healthy food
- Lots of exercise
- Meditative periods of relaxation
- Balanced nightly sleeping habits

Why Our Lifestyle is Unhealthy

When these prerequisites are established, then the metabolism works as well as for animals. Approximately 80,000 genes control and manage the processes of metabolism that are responsible for a slim body. This harmonic coordination of floral, human, and animal existence in connection with an intact environment were undisturbed for centuries and centuries - almost like the roots of a tree that reach deep into the ground and build a community with the minerals contained in them.

Today's lifestyle in western industrial countries is highly unhealthy. Exercise, less stress, and healthy foods are a relatively healthy balance for most sedentary activities.

At some point, our ancestor decided to turn away from this natural way of life. Our lifestyle today is to a high degree unnatural. The following symptoms hurt our health more and more:

- We oftentimes live almost exclusively in apartments or houses.
- Therefore, we are only exposed to temperatures that remain the same.
- We oftentimes take in only half of the oxygen that our cells need.
- We eat unhealthy foods.
- We don't exercise enough.
- We don't treat ourselves to intensive rest periods.
- We don't sleep relaxed enough, for our sleep cycles are often disturbed.

Stimulate the Slimness Genes

Our modern lifestyle has had negative influences on our bodies. If we could interpret the signals of our body correctly, we would understand what turns on the genes for a slim body:

- Exercise more outside. Don't avoid a rain shower, because it stimulates your slimness genes. It will enable your hair to grow faster, and better stimulate circulation to your skin.
- Immerse yourself once daily into deep mediation.
- Eat healthy foods.
- Create areas with different temperatures in your home.

The Consequences of a Modern Lifestyle

An unhealthy lifestyle causes numerous little changes in our body: The 80,000 active genes in the chromosomes of our cells mutate; in other words, they change. These changes are the result of bad nutrition and little exercise. Unfortunately, these warning messages of the genes are oftentimes ignored. In the beginning, it would be easy to reverse the process and return to natural - and therefore slimming - behavior patterns.

If you don't change your lifestyle substantially, your metabolism will be slowed down enormously. The consequences are far reaching:

- The hair gets thin, and falls out
- The skin wrinkles faster
- The connective tissue slackens
- Heart and circulation are weakened
- Stomach and intestinal activity slows down
- Mental symptoms of age occur
- The body weight increases continuously

Fitness and Apple Vinegar

Muscle training is not aimed at generating one's personal record by sweating and breathing profusely. Three minutes of daily exercise, held twice during the day, are enough to get the body going and promote weight loss.

Problems with heart and circulation, stomach and intestinal diseases, as well as overweight, are the most common diseases of our civilization, but hair loss and skin problems can also be caused by bad eating habits and lifestyles.

Exercise Alone is not Enough...

The right time and the right food in the form of fat-freeing biological substances are very important. Kinesiologists found out that a special combination of nutrition and exercise, such as weight-loss snacks and aerobics, is essential to increase the success of a diet by up to 30 percent. In other words: Exercise alone does not remove a single pound.

Proper Food is Also Necessary

Fitness exercises only work when combined with the right food. Examples are 50 knee-bends or sit-ups. We already described in this guide how apple vinegar before or after a meal can enhance the utilization of protein. This protein is also necessary to lose weight.

How the Genes Cause the Buildup of Muscle

Modern genetics give coaches, kinesiologists, and active athletes new insights into the metabolism of muscle cells, and therefore improve instructions for the ideal training program:

- In each cell nucleus of the 70 trillion body cells, there are 23 chromosome pairs that contain genetic information
- Each chromosome has a long string of molecules - the deoxyribonucleic acid (DNA). The DNA string of a single cell is close to 6 1/2 feet (2 meters) long. All DNA strings of a single person combined cover approximately 1,000 times the distance between the sun and earth.
- Each single string of DNA can be seen as a spiral rope ladder

with about 3,500 trillion steps. In each cell nucleus, there are 46 DNA strings.

- These strings hold approximately 80,000 genes. Some are really close, spread over less than 1,000 steps; others are far-spread, covering 100,000 steps. The longest human gene is the dystrophingne: It stretches over 2,300 trillion steps on the rope ladder of the DNA string molecule.

- This dystrophingene is responsible for the building of muscles. That is why it always takes a long time after you lift weights for the upper arms to swell. It takes 14 to 24 hours before the new muscle is visible.

The Protein-Muscle Game

- *Proteins are constantly built and reduced in muscles. Whereas, most of the 20 amino acids (proteins) take a detour via intestines and liver from the digesting food, while some long-chain amino acids approach the muscles directly.*

- *These amino acids are called leuzin, isoleuzin, and valin. The buildup of protein in the muscles is little during periods of physical activity, because the protein is partially needed to produce energy directly. It is only a few hours later that the body builds up the proteins in its muscles again.*

- *Leuzin is the typical amino acid of the muscles. It has pain-reducing powers, because it postpones the decrease of the body's own "pain killers" (endorphins). In light of our evolution, powerful and dynamic muscle work means battling, hunting, fighting and stressing out.*

- *The special built-in protein in the muscle causes fat reduction with the mitochondria. The genetic principle is: The more exercise, the more synthesis of protein in the cell. This requires vast amounts of fat, so it can be burned to create energy.*

A combination of physical activity and a healthy diet makes your diet a success. Even the best athlete does not stay slim with french fries, pizza and torts.

How Apple Vinegar and Protein Take Care of Building New Muscle

The muscle will only grow if enough muscle protein is present in the cells. If there is a lack of muscle protein, then the so-called stringent factors of the genes inside the cells' nucleus announce the lack of protein. As a consequence, the dystrophingenes immediately stop their activity. Even if you were to continue your training, not a single muscle would develop. But if there is enough protein, and a single sip of apple vinegar takes care of that, then the number of ribosomes inside the muscle cells increases rapidly. The protein molecules are built inside the ribosomes, those tiny, small protein plants. People who do not exercise very often have sometimes only 20,000 ribosomes in a single muscle cell. Trained and physically active people have over 200,000 ribosomes per cell.

To keep the muscle metabolism going, the mitochondria and ribosomes need enough fat molecules. The result of this process is, therefore, the decrease of fat cells.

Recommended Sports

A combination of anaerobic and aerobics is the ideal way to initiate the fat-reducing processes inside the body. Anaerobic include:

- Lifting weights.

Genes control the building of muscle. The command to build new muscles is only given after training over an extended period of time.

- Working with body building machines.
- Three-minute stretching.
- Three-minute gymnastics.
- Short-distance crawl (swimming).
- Climbing stairs.
- Short sprints.

Small Amounts of Fat Loss

These physical activities burn exclusively carbohydrates, or glucose, but fat is only burned in very small quantities. Therefore, these exercises stimulate many weight loss processes. The right nutrition, such as a lot of whole grain products, fresh fruit, and vegetables, is of utter importance.

Aerobics

Aerobic exercises do not have a direct influence on the adipozytes (fat cells). But short exercises of three minutes affect the slimness genes directly. These give the right orders to the cells that initiate the fat-burning processes a little later.

One of these processes can best be shown with this example:
The more glucose that is burned into energy in a muscle cell, the more mitochondria and ribosomes are generated. The consequence is an increase in the metabolism. Since glucose molecules are used up

Bodybuilders know why they add protein powder to their diet. Protein is the elementary building block for muscles. A sip of apple vinegar won't make you look like Arnold Schwartenegger, but your body will have more protein to build muscles.

quickly, the cells have a higher demand for energy. These are the fat molecules that give the muscles, especially the heart, the right power.

Aerobics - the Fat Eater

The longer one jogs, rides a bike, swims, climbs, or engages in any other activity, the more fat is burned. The better the body's stamina, the more depot fat is burned. An untrained person burns mostly glucose while hiking in the mountains. A person with greater stamina burns many fat molecules on the same hike. Aerobic exercises make losing weight easy for you. The body has, after all, over 70 trillion cells to burn the triglycerides: a great potential that can burn a great amount of fat molecules at any time.

A combination of anaerobic and aerobic exercises, or short-term and long-term exercises, are ideal, e.g., short gymnastic exercises and one or two tennis matches per week. Have a beverage containing apple vinegar before or after each meal, because the loss of weight involves the loss of protein, and that is what the acetic acid supplies to the metabolism.

What Carbohydrates Do

An old rule says: Carbohydrates make fat, protein keeps and makes slim. Foods high in carbohydrates, such as noodles, rice, bread, cake,

The body burns many carbohydrates when it is engaged in activities such as bodybuilding or sprints, but no fat is burned with such short-term activities.

or sweets, are fed into the blood via the hormone of the pancreas, the insulin. Insulin can be compared to a key that locks fat cells so no fat molecules can be set free. It is especially the glucose contained in pastries (made from lightly-colored flour) and sweets that prevent weight loss even hours after they are consumed. To lose weight through sports, one has to consume complex carbohydrates, such as those contained in whole grain bread, natural rice, potatoes, or vegetables.

Stay Away from Torts and Cakes!

One single piece of black forest cake can destroy the success of a busy training day: Scientists have calculated that the consumption of a muffin weighing 4 oz. (125 g) can cause a weight gain of 1 pound (500 g), simply because the entire metabolism is stalled. The body stores reserves, but it does not burn them. The "one-way-street fat" is built.

What Effects Nutrition Rich in Protein Has

The consumption of foods rich in protein increases the rate of metabolism. The production of hundreds of trillions of proteins requires a vast demand for energy, especially when the protein depots of the body, e.g., muscles, are empty. This can be observed when you have trouble going to sleep after a meal rich in protein. The metabolism of the cells works at optimum capacity.

The best antidotes for fat are exercises building stamina:
Riding a bike, swimming, jogging, and similar forms of exercise do not just burn
carbohydrates - here is where you sweat away excess fat.

Why Being Cold is Healthy

Being cold enhances weight loss more than sweating. Constant changes in temperature stimulate the slimness genes. Our genes - the total sum of all human genes - is identical to those of our ancestors. These ancestors, if they lived in the Stone Age, all lived in primitive quarters and were often exposed to cold. Their food consisted, therefore, mostly of rich meals. These enabled them to take in energy, and to produce body heat.

The Good Side of Goose Bumps

People today eat rich and fatty foods, and additionally consume great amounts of carbohydrates, but most people try to stay warm. The nutrition is no longer burned, but stored in fat depots. Therefore, molecular-biological experts about slimness give the following advice: Create a condition of being chilled, where the body shivers slightly, with an "irritated skin" that fights the intruding cold with goose bumps. This symptom of being chilled is a genetic relic from the olden days, when our ancestors were covered with hair; hair cells that long since have died erect themselves where once there was fur. Birds, foxes, and other animals do that, too, to retain heat when they are cold. It is then that their bodies burn a great amount of the fat stored in their fat depots. This principle is also true for humans.

- Don't avoid cold, but endure the cold for a while. Obviously, no longer than your health will allow.

The tip from experts is: More foods rich in protein and complex carbohydrates should be part of an athlete's nutrition. If you suffer from insomnia, then you should eat your last meal that is high in protein rather early (if possible, before 6 p.m.).

- Don't wait for nice weather, but go for a walk even when it rains or snows.
- Don't put on too many clothes. Rather, you should walk until you are warm.

The Body Likes it Hot and Cold

When we provide a constant body temperature with our clothes and heated rooms, then our slimness genes are rather passive. A diet in a warm environment is much less effective than one in a cold environment. Even variations of a few degrees can make a big difference. Stress hormones exclusively - like those produced when the body is chilled - have the ability to open fat cells so that fat molecules are burned.

Changes in Temperature Can Create Miracles

Changes in temperature are best to support the effect of apple vinegar on your diet. The difference in temperature forces the body to adjust to extreme changes. Such a condition of stress leads to lipolysis (fat-freeing) that will even last over a long time period.

A walk in bad weather is not very appealing, but your
body appreciates a little cold.

Lose Weight Effectively with Cold

- Hot and cold showers activate the slimness genes that immediately determine if molecules are to be burned.

- The rooms of your house or apartment should never have the same temperature. Ideally, hallways and staircases are cool, while living area and office are warm, or well-tempered. You can also create a difference in temperature between other rooms in your home and the kitchen and bathroom.

- The body is forced to adjust to constantly changing temperatures without you noticing it. This is already the case if the air of your hallway is just half a degree lower than the air in your bathroom. The skin of face and hands are the first to feel such slight differences in temperature, and our genes react within seconds.

Reminder:

These Foods Make You Fat:

- Sweet drinks such as lemonade, soda, coffee, or those that are sweetened too strongly - with a certain predisposition, also sweet fruit, or sweet fruit juices.
- Pastries made with lightly colored flour, such as noodles, white or mixed bread.
- Polished (white) rice.
- Sausage.
- Fatty meats.
- Salty-crispy skin of fried or grilled poultry.
- Fatty sauces, dressings, dip, mayonnaise.
- Fatty sweet cakes, torts, or baked goods, chocolates, or candy.
- Sweets, such as pralines.
- Ice cream, sweet creamy desserts, tiramisu, and sweet puddings.
- All alcoholic beverages, such as schnapps, liquor and sweet wines, but also beer, wine and liquor, if consumed in great quantities.
- Too much cream or fat cheese.

Foods That Make You Slim

- Fruit
- Salad
- Vegetables
- Raw Vegetables
- Whole Grain Products
- Natural Rice
- Potatoes
- Seafood
- Lean Meat
- Soy or Tofu Products
- Curd Cheese and Low-Fat Yogurt
- Low-Fat Cheese

METRIC CONVERSION CHART

Volume
Measurements (Dry)

1/8 teaspoon = 0.5 ml
1/4 teaspoon = 1 ml
1/2 teaspoon = 2 ml
3/4 teaspoon = 4 ml
1 teaspoon = 5 ml
1 tablespoon = 15 ml
2 tablespoons = 30 ml
1/4 cup = 6O ml
1/3 cup = 75 ml
1/2 cup = 125 ml
2/3 cup = 15O ml
3/4 cup = 175 ml
1 cup = 250 ml
2 cups = 1 pint = 500 ml
3 cups = 750 ml
4 cups = 1 quart = 1 L

Weights (mass)
1/2 ounce = 15 g
1 ounce = 30 g
3 ounces = 90 g
4 ounces = 120 g
8 ounces = 225 g
10 ounces = 285 g
12 ounces = 360 g
16 ounces = 1 lb. =450 g

Dimensions

1/16 inch = 2 mm
1/8 inch – 3 mm
1/4 inch = 6 mm
1/2 inch = 1.5 cm
3/4 inch = 2 cm
1 inch = 2.5 cm

Oven Temperatures
250°F = 120°C
275°F = 140°C
300°F = 150°C
325°F = 160°C
350°F = 180°C
375°F = 190°C
400°F = 200°C
425°F = 220°C
450°F = 230°C

Volume Measurements (fluid)

1 fluid ounce (2 tablespoons) = 30 ml
4 fluid ounces (1/2 cup) = 125 ml
8 fluid ounces (1 cup) = 250 ml
12 fluid ounces (1 1/2 cups) = 375 ml
16 fluid ounces (2 cups) = 500 ml

BAKING PAN SIZES

Utensil	Size in Inches/Quarts	Metric Volume	Size in Centimeters
Baking or Cake Pan (square or rectangular)	8 x 8 x 2	2 L	20 x 20 x 5
	9 x 9 x 2	2.5 L	22 x 22 x 5
	12 x 8 x 2	3 L	30 x 20 x 5
	13 x 9 x 2	3.5 L	33 x 23 x 5
Loaf Pan	8 x 4 x 3	1.5 L	20 x 10 x 7
	9 x 5 x 3	2 L	23 x 13 x 7
Round Layer Cake Pan	8 x 1 1/2	1.2 L	20 x 4
	9 x 1 1/2	1.5 L	23 x 4
Pie Plate	8 x 1 1/2	750 ml	20 x 3
	9 x 1 1/2	1.5 L	23 x 4
Baking Dish Or Casserole	1 quart	1 L	- - -
	1 1/2 quarts	1.5 L	- - -
	2 quarts	2 L	- - -

Recipe Index

Index